'Catherine Taylor's memoir *The Stirrings* is a dark, wry tribute to the Steel City, and her encounters with many of its best-known inhabitants . . . A vivid chronicle of a young woman's journey into adulthood, and an equally vivid portrait of a place and moment in time' *Telegraph*

'Part poignant memoir of time and place. Part record of the violence, and indifference, against which most girls grow up. *The Stirrings* is a pleasure and a shock'

Eimear McBride

'A coming-of-age memoir which charts the author's experiences growing up in 1970s and 80s Sheffield, the evocation of time and place is so good you are almost surprised when you look up and see you are elsewhere'

i news

'From chlorine and Quavers to the Jesus and Mary Chain, an engaging personal and political 1980s awakening'

Richard Beard

'Catherine Taylor's account of her youth is a lyrical study of how place shapes character . . . Assured and perceptive . . . She brilliantly evokes the "tiny traumas" of childhood . . . The reader may wish this memoir were longer'

Observer

The Stirrings

A Memoir in Northern Time

CATHERINE TAYLOR

WEIDENFELD & NICOLSON

First published in Great Britain in 2023 by Weidenfeld & Nicolson
This paperback edition published in 2024 by Weidenfeld & Nicolson,
an imprint of The Orion Publishing Group Ltd
Carmelite House, 50 Victoria Embankment
London EC4Y 0DZ

An Hachette UK Company

3 5 7 9 10 8 6 4 2

A CIP catalogue record for this book is
available from the British Library.

ISBN (Mass Market Paperback 978 1 4746 2531 9
ISBN (eBook) 978 1 4746 2532 6
ISBN (Audio) 978 1 4746 2533 3

Typeset by Born Group
Printed and bound in Great Britain by Clays Ltd, Elcograf S.p.A.

www.weidenfeldandnicolson.co.uk
www.orionbooks.co.uk

In memory of L.M.H. 1969–1991
and for S.P.T.

Maen braf yn yr haf

Catherine Taylor was born in Waikato, Aotearoa New Zealand, and grew up in Sheffield, South Yorkshire. Formerly publisher at The Folio Society and deputy director of English PEN, she is now a freelance writer, critic, and editor. Her essays have appeared in *Granta*, *Aeon*, and the collection *Trauma: Art and Mental Health* (Dodo Ink, 2021). She edited *The Book of Sheffield: A City in Short Fiction* (Comma Press, 2019), chosen as the 2020 Big City Read by Sheffield Libraries. She lives in London. This is her first book.

Poppies whose roots are in man's veins
Drop, and are ever dropping;
But mine in my ear is safe—
Just a little white with the dust.

Isaac Rosenberg, 'Break of Day in the Trenches'

This is a work of autobiography entirely from my own perspective and allowing for the elisions and imperfections of memory.

Prologue

They say witches float. Late afternoon, late after school, late November, late in the year. I am late for tea. Although my mother is still at work, a peanut butter sandwich wrapped in tinfoil and a Kit Kat await me on a plate on the kitchen table, to scoff while ostensibly doing homework or, the more likely scenario, lying on the dining-room floor, eyes closed, Siouxsie and the Banshees on the record player. Refracting, edgy beats matched by dolefully menacing lyrics, telling me that the house is happy, all is well, and that there is no hell.

Except there is hell, and it is here, it is surrounding us. The misty drizzle is replete with it. Five girls stand on Montague Street in Sharrow, at the eastern end of the old General Cemetery. It is past dusk or twilight – no one knows the difference – on a Friday afternoon, five o'clock. The end of the first year of a new decade, the first year of the tenacious grip of Margaret Thatcher's Conservative government and the industrial unrest that will mark the next few years. In Sheffield, known as the Steel City, 1980 has been marked by the national steelworkers' strike which has seen workers out picketing and clashing with police in a vain attempt to save jobs in an industry under threat.

We are thirteen: a glittering, dangerous age. We are not supposed to be here. We are spotty but invincible, and also bored, an admixture which has brought us to the corner of this abandoned place, away from warm sitting rooms with the hiss of gas fires and *Sapphire and Steel* on the telly. Our school uniforms – a muddy dark brown – are each subtly customised, as much as we dare, for our teachers are self-important in their scrutiny. Rain trickles into the open hood of my duffle coat and down my neck. We are suspicious of each other, and silent. On Fridays the school day finishes at lunchtime; it is that sort of school. But there had been another murder at the beginning of the week, of a student in Leeds, an hour away from Sheffield. The killings, which began when we were small children, so that we have grown up alongside them as if they are our shadow selves, are increasing, as are the attacks on women and girls walking alone. A new name added to the list read out on the radio and TV bulletins, another blurred photograph printed in the newspapers. The names and photographs are of somebody's daughter, mother, wife, sister, friend. Those who escape are the 'lucky' ones. Somehow, they got away from the man I see in nightmares. And although he does not appear in human form, I instinctively know it is him. The Ripper.

At night, as I sleep, he manifests at first as a small black dot in an otherwise untroubled sky, like an eye mote at the border of vision. The dot increases in size, metamorphosing in shape with alarming rapidity, until my sight is overwhelmed by a huge, oily-feathered bird coming in for the kill. I usually wake up just at the moment when my face is covered and blotted out, my mouth stuffed full of soft black feathers.

As autumn proceeds, the afternoons growing shorter and the nights longer, a quiet panic has begun to set in among our parents. Therefore on this Friday we are not allowed to become our weekend, individual selves – not yet. Instead, we are collected at the school gate in assorted bundles and ferried to each other's houses in cars or on buses or on foot.

The group I am with, randomly assembled, has little to say to each other; an unnatural and awkward collective. We spend a couple of desultory hours flicking through old copies of *Jackie* and *Smash Hits*, outwardly scornful of the urgent anxieties expressed in the former through anguished letters printed on the 'Dear Cathy and Claire' problem page: *How can I make him like me? Can you get pregnant the first time?* In reality we are completely naive in terms of our own experience. Mostly we speculate on where the Ripper will appear next – for it was of course he who had committed the latest murder.

Despite the fact that it took place in a different city, the proximity, the electric terror sparked and magnified each time he strikes in towns and cities across Yorkshire, is substantial. It also inflames something else: rebellion. And so, this late afternoon, we sneak, by tacit agreement and in single file, through the kitchen and out the back door onto the indifferently lit, rain-slicked streets of Broomhall.

This particular street appears blandly innocuous: comfortable Victorian villas like the one from which we emerge, with protective trees and huge hidden gardens: but its outer edges, towards the ring road and town, nearer Havelock Square and Hanover Street, are a mix of terraces, bedsits, run-down flats; the area known as the 'red-light district'. Much of it will be demolished in 1982. The vast bulk of Viners, at the corner of Broomhall Road and Hanover Way, is also doomed – by the economic downturn and cheaper imports from abroad. Once the biggest cutlery factory not only in Sheffield but the whole of the UK, the firm will go bankrupt in 1985.

As we slink like cats from street lamp to street lamp we pass a couple of women standing at the corner of where Broomhall Road meets Victoria Road, waiting blankly in the rain for a car to slow down. They look cold in their thin jackets and skimpy skirts. We stare, frankly, although we aren't supposed to look. These are the women whom the press and police vilify. The so-called 'good-time girls'. They don't seem to be having a good time, to me. They look tired, resigned, and vulnerable.

We continue, crossing the busy main road, and then up an ominously quiet and empty Montague Street.

Ahead of us is a long path winding through the cemetery which, as I inform the others – it being my foolish and ingratiating suggestion that we come here, my contribution to the group – leads to catacombs, and a deserted church. Bordered on either side by a dense forest of gravestones, it is shadowy in the murk. Somewhere to the left beyond the trees a spooky walled-up chapel surveys its clammy kingdom. The imposing Egyptian-style gatehouse, thick columns sculpted on either side with two snakes, their tails in their mouths, marks the exit to Cemetery Avenue – less than ten minutes' walk and many pounding heartbeats away. There might be skulls, and other severed body parts lurking amid the undergrowth: a large number of the graves are smashed and broken. There are certainly hundreds of dead people underneath our feet. Beside us is Stalker Walk and the Porter Brook river, where, one winter a few years before, out with my mother, I saw a kingfisher flashing by in a whirr of blue and green. 'It means the halcyon days are coming,' she told me, but whatever the halcyon days were, they had not come. Instead, my father had left us not long after.

Having consumed only half a Twix since lunchtime, I think longingly of my peanut butter sandwich growing stale on our kitchen table, and the new season of *Dallas* due to begin that evening, which my mother and I like to watch together as a Friday-night ritual. My brother recently went away to university in London; the house feels big and lonely. Tomorrow is Saturday, the day of the dreaded fortnightly 'access' visit with my father. I prefer not to think beyond *Dallas*.

It had seemed a good idea to break up the boredom and frustration of the afternoon and also to defy our parents, just for an hour. We aren't supposed to be out alone once it gets dark. One of us quietly sings that old song about a killer on the road, and we giggle nervously, fidgeting in the cold. Someone else lets off an extravagant burp. My voice embarrassingly thin and pleading, I suggest diverting back to the streets, to get chips on nearby Sharrow Vale Road, but Lucy has a different idea. She is one of the self-elected ringleaders of our form, along with her sidekick Nina. The pair terrorises the leaden minutes before registration each morning, posturing at the front of the classroom, heaping humiliation on anyone deemed unpopular or shy.

Nina isn't part of this afternoon's group, so their poisonous dual effect has been somewhat neutralised by her absence, but now Lucy is beginning to enjoy herself. She possesses all the hauteur of a Marie Antoinette in training. *They say witches float – if you throw them into water –* this directed at me (we are studying Arthur Miller's *The Crucible* and it has left an enthusiastic impression). *Shall we give it a go?*

There is a horrified, excited pause. No one speaks either to corroborate or dismiss the suggestion, and for one long, icy moment I picture myself being marched to the scene of my execution, the kingfisher – now posing as a harbinger of doom – appearing to smirk at me from a safe distance. Then, an intervention. *Don't be daft*, Anna says, mildly, and Lucy narrows her already narrow eyes and flicks her

6

annoying ponytail: *I was only joking, idiot.* The others titter anxiously. We brace ourselves as Lucy, affecting nonchalance, weighs up the situation, the only sound the steady drip of the rain from tree branches that can by now scarcely be made out in the gloom. After some deliberation: *Let's have a dare.* Lucy's white teeth flash momentarily, like a switchblade cutting through the semi-darkness. We are to run through the vigilant stillness of the cemetery and out the other side. Whoever's last has to buy chips as forfeit. We'll show the Ripper we're not afraid of him. *Bloody FUCKING Jack the Ripper* – the last emphasised with care by Lucy, savouring the forbidden swear words.

She points at me with a stabbing action: *You first, or are you too frit?* I freeze. An uncomfortable pause. Again, to my surprise, Anna comes to my rescue. '*You suggested it,*' she says to Lucy. '*Why don't you go first?*' Hesitation, but Lucy cannot back out now. Another toss of the ponytail switch. *Count to ten and then the next one follow me . . .* and she is off, her long legs and that swinging bell of hair quickly disappearing from view as the path darkens before her, before us all.

One by one those remaining run in the direction Lucy has gone, scattering as deer from an invisible hunter. Their breath hangs in the chilly air like ectoplasm. Left alone, I shiver on the cemetery's periphery. I am afraid of the dark. Some nights I sleep with my childhood lava lamp on, its reassuring hyperactive glow standing between me and the blackness beyond. Now, as I try to move forward, a strange paralysis seems to creep up my legs as if twisting ropes of ivy are surging out of the earth beneath, binding me to the spot.

There is nothing and no one in front of me; the longer the delay the more likely that the others will not wait. The Porter Brook rushes on obliviously somewhere to the right. Ahead is not to be contemplated. Behind, Montague Street – with its car park and few office buildings – is deserted, one lone, wan street lamp flickering on and off like a half-hearted signal. The lights and traffic of the main road – Ecclesall Road, at the very far end of which is my house – are increasingly faint.

A loud crack interrupts the silence: a branch bending under the weight of water. Or the tread of a foot, snapping a twig, and a blunt instrument swinging by the side of a figure as yet unseen.

The invisible ivy tendrils loosen from my immobilised legs.

Now I can run, but not forward, into the black hole of the cemetery. I will not complete the dare. I have failed. At registration on Monday morning there will be ridicule, which will be deserved, because I am *frit*. Turning back, wheezing and sobbing in painful gasps, a stitch in my side, I race downhill to Ecclesall Road, merging gratefully with the rush-hour crowds. I visualise the others bitching about my cowardice. Sprinkling salt and vinegar onto hot greasy chips, linking arms, their mocking refrain of 'Riders on the Storm' fading into the night as they saunter down Sharrow Vale Road.

Chapter One

Pre-history

The summer of 1976 was the hottest in Britain since records began. As well as the intense, endless heat, the sweltering nation endured a severe water shortage, standpipes in the streets, and a plague of ladybirds moving across the UK's cities and towns. During those drought-heavy weeks, the water levels of Derbyshire's Ladybower reservoir shrank so low that long-submerged secrets were revealed. The ruins of Derwent village, which, along with its neighbour Ashopton, had been evacuated and drowned in 1945 to make way for the creation of Ladybower, rose up through the water like a ghostly revenant. Seeking relief from the heat of Sheffield, my family drove past the reservoir one evening, the moors too parched to visit during the day. One building, partially re-emerged from the watery depths, resembled a warning finger, pointing towards something I wasn't yet able to see.

1976 would be the last summer of our family as it existed up to that point. A typical family and an ordinary story, although neither the family nor the story seems commonplace when it is your family and your story.

At school, I was relentlessly unpopular, in an imprecise way. But after that year something much more compelling and unsavoury would replace the general apathy and animosity – at least when taken apart in the busy hands of my peers – when I achieved the singular honour of being the first person in my class whose parents had split up.

I did say that mine was an ordinary story.

That long scorching summer turned out to be the dividing line between an all-too-brief before and a vast, messy after. It remains filtered through a syrupy haze. The faultless past and the compromised present are, I've found, unreliable lenses through which to view the world. What is certain is that I recall the years before 1976 only in fragments and impressions, without a fixed chronology. The period that followed hardened my perception, while simultaneously blurring the outlines I had presumed were solid. By the time I was old enough to ask *what really happened?* the once-familiar faces had altered. Some had turned away for good.

Any excavator of personal history must assume the role of private investigator into their own life. I have always loved detective stories. When I was very young, just before bedtime, I would sit, wrapped in my dressing gown, with my father while he sipped his one glass of sherry or beer, and watch American shows on television: *Hawaii Five-o*, *Kojak*, *McMillan & Wife*, *Ironside* and our favourite, *Columbo*.

The last intrigued me most because of its inverted narrative structure: the perpetrator of the crime is revealed to the audience at the opening of each episode. It is left to the perennially and deceptively rumpled detective Lieutenant Columbo to go backwards; examine the variables, work out the formula – like a masterclass in algebra – and in that way apprehend the criminal.

In my own unearthing I am both investigator and culprit.

To start at the beginning, or at a beginning.

Light. Pointing fingers of harsh bright sunlight inserted themselves through vertical slats of metal. They were seeking me out. They were all I was aware of. I raised my hands instinctively to pat and catch this light, but it was elusive, if pleasingly warm.

Nothing else, then, until a tremendous movement, a rocking. A strong smell of coal tar, a sense of propulsion, of purpose. Air composed of sticky salt spray. Many voices, tumbling over each other, and laughter. Exclamations. '*Bella Caterina!*'

Then quiet. The hot sun, the Pacific light, the rocking movement, the multitudes, all vanished, and I was looking up at a windmill on a red and gold autumn afternoon, the air now chilly and smoky, crisp leaves under my pushchair. It was late September in Essex, England. I was two and a half years old. We had travelled all the way across the world by Italian ship from New Zealand, where I was born. We had arrived.

Still only slivers of memory, sharp shards. A house near a pig farm, the animals a jumbling, snorting, stinking mass of pink, on an incline called Inkerman Hill in Buckinghamshire. My eldest brother was building a go-kart in the garage. There were apple trees in the garden, and the house had a name, not a number – Orchard View. I turned three, and a tricycle magically appeared on the front lawn. My mother, answering the telephone to someone, said, jiggling the receiver, 'I was just thinking about you.' Did thinking conjure a person up? Before many more years had passed I would learn that it did not, no matter how concentrated the effort.

I was starting to write. While my mother was busy, I scrawled my three initials over and over again on my doll, and then on anything else I could make my imprint upon.

This was not our house, it was temporary. We were in England because my father had something called a 'sabbatical'. After six months he went back to New Zealand. I thought we would all return too, although I no longer remembered the bungalow in Waikato, or our black and white cat; just that powerful light and heat. In England we had no cat, but a tortoise called Abraham. There was an electrical thunderstorm one night while my father was away and all four of us children huddled in the big bed with our mother.

A year passed in this new country; it was autumn again. In New Zealand I was born in autumn, but in England my birthday was in spring. This upside-down fact made no sense to me. Our suitcases and boxes were loaded into a car and we drove away from the apple trees, the lovely dip in which the house was set, and – to my secret relief – the pigs, all the way up the M1 motorway north to Sheffield. My father was still in New Zealand, serving out his notice at Waikato University, but he had a new job in this unknown city. It was left to my mother to sort out finding a house and schools. My sister, the oldest, a veteran of many moves, stayed behind in Buckinghamshire to start sixth form.

At the initial approach to Sheffield from the M1, the enormous twin cooling towers of Tinsley Viaduct rose from the mist like two mythical beasts. Ominous on that first occasion, I could not know that they would soon become a welcome sign of home. Sheffield was grey, grim, and wet: steep roads, forbidding buildings. Our house was very cold. Coal for the fire was kept in a special cubby-hole behind the back door, and came off onto my fingers, soft and very, very black. Stone crags loomed at the end of our road, Den Bank Drive in Crosspool. The city was entirely surrounded by moors and gritstone edges, covered with heaps of dry bracken in autumn and winter and, from June, glowing with purple heather. The back garden of the house bulged with rhubarb. We ate a lot of rhubarb. I did not especially like rhubarb. The room I slept in upstairs at the front had a bed that rocked like the ship on which we came to England. At first light every morning I would hear the milkman's van gliding along the street and the clink of milk bottles placed on doorsteps. This was how I knew another night had gone by.

Christmas Eve: first sight of snow, and my sister was coming home for the holiday. I had a bad toothache and we were all waiting, longing, for her to arrive, because then the toothache would stop, I would stop crying and Christmas would begin. I imagined my sister, with her waist-length hair and long belted winter coat from C&A, carrying a suitcase full of presents, walking though the deep snow all the way to Sheffield from Buckinghamshire, sinking into the drifts. Her glasses had steamed up in the cold. The lamps were on in the street outside and I was distracted – toothache temporarily forgotten – by the blank whiteness, its silent perfection, punctured with the criss-cross marks of birds and small animals. Later, half asleep in bed: out of nowhere carol singers outside started singing 'The First Noel'.

Little interrupted the hermetic seal of family. I had no real knowledge of the world outside, although it was beginning to intrude, sometimes in unexpectedly violent ways. One afternoon my father and I were standing at the bus shelter in Pinstone Street in the city centre, when a woman wearing a tight leather jacket and gloves crashed her motorcycle into the back of a stationary van, right next to us. The woman's helmet was wrenched off by the impact of the collision, her bright auburn hair spilling out, swiftly becoming saturated with blood. I stared, fascinated, at the flow of colours, like the ones I mixed in my paint jar, and at the abruptly unseeing eyes, even as my father picked me up and rushed me away.

A troubling viral infection on my right wrist. *Herpes simplex*, an unlovely, thick bracelet of raised, pus-filled blisters. At the Children's Hospital a doctor stuck a needle directly into the centre of the chaos. As I opened my mouth to scream in protest my mother popped a Polo mint into it.

Like most small children, my routine fears had elements of both rationality and illogic. Nightscapes were filled with fierce and violent dreams; too afraid to go to sleep, I would lie rigid in bed rocking my head from side to side and singing. I named this comforting process 'nid-nodding', convinced that something unspeakably nasty awaited me in unconsciousness.

Most of all, I feared other children. Despite our many likenesses – which included snotty noses, grazed knees, and similar-sized bodies – I knew that if a general enemy existed, it was within this mass of small humans. I was now five, and had started 'proper' school. In the playground the boys 'encouraged' us girls to show them our knickers by chasing us and pricking our cold bare legs all over with holly leaves.

Feral speaks to feral, even when disguised in party dresses and ribbons. The mysterious and uncontrollable rites of children often occurred at seemingly innocuous birthday gatherings. Those first forays into party land were tiny traumas. At one such party – at which I was, for once, wearing the correct (long) party dress for that year's fashion, with a pattern of small violet flowers on a white background, and a thin strip of purple velvet underneath the bodice – the children – all girls – were sent to play

15

'nicely' in the garden. The birthday girl led us away from the neat lawn and flower beds, up a less cultivated path towards the back wall, occupied by a scattering of garden tools, a watering can, and a compost heap. The house seemed far, far below us. As if already prepared and waiting, a ceramic basin had been placed prominently on the ground. One by one, in total silence, almost by telepathy or prearranged mutual consent, each little girl carefully lifted her impeccably ironed dress, pulled down her white underpants, and, without preamble, emptied the contents of her bowels into the bowl, one shining brown turd coiled on top of the other, like a foul-smelling serpent. I was transfixed. No one spoke, although it was indicated that my turn was next. As I countered feebly, an adult voice broke through the trance, calling from the kitchen door for us to come and wash our hands for tea. Without looking back, the others ran down to the house, with me trailing disconsolately behind, feeling, not for the first time, that I had failed some important test.

Years later, I wondered: was that bowl still there, the excrement fossilised, the motive eternally obscure.

By this time we had moved to Ranmoor, and my dream house, for the number on the door was the same as the day of my birthday. The attics were huge, big enough for my brothers to run a giant Scalextric car track the length of one room. In the back garden, a millstone – the symbol of the surrounding Peak District – leant against a wall. A giant stone circle with a hole in the middle, it dated from the nineteenth century, when it would have been used in a water mill to grind grains into flour. The millstone's appearance in our garden was a reminder of that past; I used it as a peephole. More prosaically, my father grew white roses, hollyhocks, foxgloves, and an angry-looking plant called a red-hot poker, the blazing red and yellow flowers of which I was too scared to approach in case they burned me. At the garden's far end, blue forget-me-nots ran wild and I lifted up large rocks to watch the beetles and woodlice scuttle for shelter.

Now aged seven, I had more independence, and the 'Charley Says' public information cartoon on TV urged us not to talk to strangers. Across the road from our house a narrow, leafy gennel ran alongside the Bull's Head pub where my father liked to go for a pint. I would skip, blissfully and importantly alone, down the gennel to the sweetshop, clutching the sixpences which the tooth fairy left under my pillow with happy regularity. The sweets lay in glorious wait in large old-fashioned glass jars, fetched down from high shelves and carefully dropped with tongs into tiny three-cornered paper bags which resembled minuscule hats for scaled-down sailors. Penny chews and black jacks, chocolate cigarettes, liquorice and sherbet dabs, pear drops and fizz bombs all helped to rot my baby teeth. Once, snooping through my mother's jewellery box, I had been startled to find a row of small, bloody fangs placed on cotton-wool balls as if they were precious stones.

After a bus ride, we reached school via a shortcut up sunless and silent Frog Walk, running alongside the General Cemetery, the site of future teenage terror. The

Walk always seemed claustrophobic, twisty, endless. I held tightly to the hand of the adult I was with.

Learning to read to myself was a revelation: now I could fully inhabit my own world. I was three *Wide Range Readers* ahead of the rest of the class, I was not being 'challenged' enough, and, after visiting a dark, cold building and writing the answers to some questions on a sheet of paper (apparently known as an entrance exam), I was told that a new school awaited. On the first day, my mother walked into the classroom with me and introduced me to the assembled girls. There were no boys in this school, I noticed. In that moment I was acutely aware of my mother's accent, which had never sounded less English. Once she had left, the reaction to this awkward entrance was mostly antagonistic. That hostility would be there, in one form or another, for the next nine years.

Despite school there was our family, our house, our garden. There were weekends in Derbyshire, playing on the stepping stones at Padley Gorge, and trekking up Monsal Dale. Whitsuntide brought a reminder that Derbyshire was once a pagan place. In early summer, the annual well-dressings unique to the county appeared throughout its villages. The wells would be decorated with scenes composed out of vibrant flower petals: in ancient times these served as offerings to the water gods. Over Stanage Edge we watched the hang gliders swoop like giant birds, and in Hathersage churchyard visited Robin Hood's sidekick Little John's surprisingly capacious burial place. In Castleton we climbed the steep path to the ruin of Peveril Castle and visited the underground limestone cavern, where the semi-precious mineral known as Blue John is found. At Eyam, the village that shut its doors to the outside world in 1665 when the plague arrived in a parcel of cloth from London, the crosses marked on the doors of the doomed cottages could still be seen. All of this ignited my nascent imagination.

Whatever the weather, my mother packed a cold bacon-and-egg pie and a thermos of orange squash, and we sat on the rough grass picnicking among the sheep droppings, our hair vertical and eyes watering in the fierce wind blowing across the moors.

The 1970s were inching forward. At sixteen, my eldest brother left school, cut off his much-disapproved-of long hair, put on a suit and got a job in town at Cole Brothers' department store in Barker's Pool, near to Josephine's nightclub, where my parents sometimes went to 'dinner dances'. I envisaged them on these occasions gyrating while somehow manoeuvring the trays in their hands, piled high with food and drink. My sister, meanwhile, had started at Sheffield University, and was living with us again, stylish in a navy-blue PVC maxi-coat which crackled when she moved, Mary Quant sparkling nail varnish to match, and wide trousers known as 'Oxford bags'. She and her friends took me to see Nana Mouskouri sing at Sheffield City Hall, opposite Coles. For the performance everyone sat on orange scatter cushions on the floor. 'Is this your kid?' someone asked my sister during the evening. I was alarmed. Was I? 'No.'

Apparently school wasn't enough in terms of social activity and I needed to 'join in' more. The Brownies, which I attended weekly, was not a success. The badges I was compelled to acquire – Housekeeping, Needlework – seemed even at the age of seven or eight to hold diminishing returns, and I lost my eyebrows after an ill-judged candle placement at the December Christingle service. One spring afternoon, at the end of the school day, walking home from the bus stop with my mother, she told me that she was going to leave her job as a schoolteacher in Walkley and open a bookshop, an ambition which had flickered since she was a child growing up in rural New Zealand. Although I liked the thought of having more access to books (we went each week to Broomhill Library), I was worried. Midweek evenings were devoted to swimming at Heeley baths, near the school where my mother taught. The tang of chlorine and synthetic taste of cheesy Quavers from the vending machine were inexpressibly bound up with Heeley: no other pool would ever come close to that first tentative immersion.

Preoccupied, I neglected to listen to the rest of what my mother was saying. Turning the corner into our road, I experienced the shock of a 'For Sale' sign outside our house. The sign, an aberration, had definitely not been there that morning. My mother explained that in order to buy the shop premises we would have to sell our house and move somewhere cheaper. This betrayal – I could view it in no other terms – had clearly been planned for a while. Our house – *my* house, where I assumed I would live always, even when grown up – would instead belong to another family. A different child would fossick around among my forget-me-not patch at the end of the garden, sleep in my bedroom, roam the attics. For the first time, I actually hated my parents. Sullen and powerless, when prospective buyers came round I refused to tidy my room, glaring at them through a curtain of deliberately unwashed hair.

Even so, the house was sold. The new house was at Hunter's Bar, directly opposite Endcliffe Park. Tall, thin, Edwardian, with spooky cobwebbed cellars, and a sundial in the back yard. At dawn on cold, misty May Day mornings – my mother's birthday – at exactly five o'clock, a team of Morris dancers with their bells, swords and handkerchiefs would welcome the Beltane at the park's entrance.

We didn't have money to change the décor, so it remained the same for all the years we lived in that house, including the rough and resilient Tintawn sisal carpets we had brought with us from Ranmoor and tacked through every room, even the bathroom. Doors painted dark purple, loud wallpaper, and stained glass in the inner door of the front porch. The blind at my bedroom window was decorated with a print of giant green and purple grapes, resembling a cluster of haemorrhoids. The window faced an outhouse in the dark recesses of the garden. Scrambling up a steep rocky patch, I would perch on its roof, looking up through the leaves of the trees that sentinelled the surrounding high wall and back again at the house, feeling apart and together all at once. I had a swing of my own, a compensation for moving from Ranmoor, and would rock for hours back and forth, singing the most morbid hymns from my electric blue *Songs of Praise* school hymn book, alternated with current chart hits such as Abba's 'Fernando'.

On Thursdays I was allowed to watch *Top of the Pops*. When Queen reached Number 1 in the summer of 1975 with 'Bohemian Rhapsody' I obsessed over the video of Freddie Mercury: his white suit with the fringes on the sleeves, his graceful piano playing, dark hair, and beautiful eyelashes. I would marry him, I decided, if I had not already married our sixteen-year-old family friend, Vincent. At my sister's twenty-first birthday party that autumn, Vincent, in very tight jeans, had struck some impressive disco moves, a contrast to the rest of the gathering – the men with full beards, women with long, middle-parted hair and maxi dresses, all swaying back to back in our creaking attic to Fleetwood Mac's 'Albatross'. At that age I was oblivious to the idea that both Freddie's and Vincent's romantic interests might lie elsewhere.

Time was ticking down now, fast and faster. None of us were aware of this, of course.

During the stultifying heat of that summer of 1976, Elton John and Kiki Dee dominated the radio with 'Don't Go Breaking My Heart': easy to recognise this now as a premonition.

My sister was living with her boyfriend. My eldest brother had moved into a squat at the top of the ironically named Park Lane in Broomhall. Once, visiting the day after a particularly wild party, I noticed there was no longer a front door to the house. Ripped off its hinges, it was now propped casually against the outside wall. This disarray troubled me, a violence which seemed against the natural order of things.

In August, to escape the ferocious heatwave of that summer, and minus my two eldest siblings who had long since made their own holiday arrangements, we drove up to Scotland. The sky was still light at ten o'clock when we took the ferry from Oban to Mull, with its otters and endless white beaches. Excited to discover the main town was called Tobermory, I informed anyone who would listen that it must be named after one of The Wombles. We mooched along the sand, or slithered around rock pools. My mother held up a towel to protect my modesty on the deserted beach while I wriggled in and out of swimming togs. She rubbed Nivea Creme – the scent of which would remind me of her forever – into my skin to prevent sunburn.

My father, famously, was not keen on beach holidays. Most of that trip, he chose to sit in the car rather than join us on the shore. One particularly hot day, I looked back at him, one arm resting out of the car window, shirt sleeves rolled up to the elbow. His right arm was the only part of him ever to turn brown. Eyes covered by dark sunglasses, he was listening to the car radio, or maybe just staring into space. He seemed very far away.

Back in Sheffield, the weather, at last cooler, drifted into autumn.

Sunday afternoon. My mother was busy in the back attic, headscarf on, cleaning the windows, when the loose frame of one slipped, and the lower sash crashed down on her hands. In pain and shock, she called out to my father, weeding the garden directly below. On the next floor down, looking out of the window underneath the attic, I could see exactly what my mother saw: my father apparently ignoring her calls for help. I sensed her increasing panic, but my father did not turn round. He didn't appear to even hear her, impossible given how close he was, until I shouted for him and finally, slowly, he reacted.

That Christmas I was given a dressing gown; red wool, with wooden ladybirds for buttons. It was the first which wasn't a hand-me-down from my brothers. The buttons would remind me of the ladybird plagues of the hot summer just past each time I carefully fastened one. The odd atmosphere in our family persisted: it had not been killed off by the chill of winter. The only other recollection I have of that Christmas is of my father's inexplicably bad mood, and me crying.

The year ended. The hourglass of our family had a few grains of sand left in it, only a few. The white sands of Mull, the soggy sands of day trips to Lincolnshire, the forgotten black volcanic sands of New Zealand, to which, in early January, my mother and I would be travelling for the first time in nearly a decade.

Nothing could be known. When we returned to England, everything would change.

Chapter Two

Jubilee

The year of the Queen's Silver Jubilee, of street parties and commemorations and flag waving, was also the year of the rise of the subculture known as punk: the mainstream and boring versus the exciting and unpredictable. 'God Save the Queen' sneered The Sex Pistols' Johnny Rotten, to the nation's mingled panic and ecstasy. The music, with its shouted lyrics and urgent discord, was jarring and angry. I recall little about the street parties of 1977, but I do remember the visceral jolt that was punk music, along with its look: the ripped jeans and fishnet tights, the safety pins ornamenting ears: a new anti-style with Derbyshire teacher turned fashion designer Vivienne Westwood at its helm. As the year went on, and my family circumstances drastically altered, I became jarring and angry, too.

My parents had met in 1952, the same year Elizabeth II ascended the throne. Following two years of hated National Service in England, my father had emigrated to Australia in 1950, buying a government-subsidised assisted migration passage from England to Australia for the sum of ten pounds. People who took part in this scheme were known as the 'Ten Pound Poms'. My mother, who grew up on a small dairy farm in Kaukapakapa, north-west of Auckland, had been hitchhiking with a friend around Australia after finishing teacher-training college. My parents' first encounter was on a boat from Australia to New Zealand, where my mother was immediately intrigued by the strikingly handsome young man with curly dark hair and high cheekbones, sitting on deck reading G.D.H. Cole's book *The Intelligent Man's Guide to the Post-War World*. By the end of the short voyage, they were engaged. 1977, then, was the year of my parents' own personal jubilee.

On 4 February of that anniversary year, Fleetwood Mac released their now-classic break-up album *Rumours*. On 5 February, a twenty-eight-year-old woman named Irene Richardson, who was in such a bad financial situation that she had put her small son into care and was living in a public toilet, was murdered in the Chapeltown area of Leeds. The murder had occurred at almost the exact spot where twenty-year-old Marcella Claxton had been violently attacked on her way home from a party the year before. Marcella, who needed fifty stitches to her head, survived the assault; her four-month pregnancy did not. Police also began to make links between the killing of Irene Richardson and two previous murders in Chapeltown, those of Wilma McCann and Emily Jackson, along with attempts on the lives of at least three other women, including Marcella Claxton. They were, they now believed, looking for a serial killer.

28

After the Christmas holiday, I had not returned to school. Instead, as the optimistically named spring term began in early January, my mother and I travelled on a succession of aeroplanes, nearly twelve thousand miles away from our home in Sheffield, to New Zealand, a country I had last seen when I was two and a half, and which I barely remembered. We were to be away for two months, staying with relatives and friends in and around Auckland and Hamilton; the dismal British winter swapped for a subtropical South Pacific summer. I was as unaware of national and international news as I was of what might or might not be happening in Sheffield, or the reason why my mother and I had left home, and for so long. Although we were now on the other side of the world, the Jubilee and the Queen followed us. From late February into March, *she* was on tour there, a little bit of Britain we had been unable to escape.

I was nine, and this unusual caesura was presented as an adventure, a delicious sun-filled pause in normal life. I was freed from the confines of school, although I had Maths and English exercises and a weekly 'newsletter' to mail to my teachers and class back in Sheffield. I was deliberately reticent in this newsletter. New Zealand was mine, not theirs. I did not write about Mount Maunganui, a sacred Māori site and a surfing beach with brilliant white sands, or the sandbar off which I learnt to pluck *pipis* – edible shellfish that washed up in their hundreds – straight out of the water breaking onto the shore. I would prise open the *pipis'* hinged shells like tiny jewel boxes, to reveal bivalves eaten raw, or cooked over a barbecue, savouring their salty, slippery texture on the tongue. In my clipped missives to school I also neglected to mention Narrow Neck Beach, situated directly across from the extinct volcano of Rangitoto Island. Nor did I write about Piha, near the Waitākere Ranges, presided over by a rock, millions of years old, in the shape of a lion's head, its sands black with powdery volcanic ash, its surfers drawn to the towering waves, or the sandflies that accosted us there as soon as we left the protection of the car.

I did write, in no doubt overly earnest prose, about the vast blackness of the subtropical sky at night, a springy, velvet pincushion pierced with tiny pinheads of silver stars, from which I could easily pick out the Southern Cross. I wrote too about the weekend spent fishing on my uncle's boat, when a tug at the end of the line I was concentratedly holding led to the hauling in of a two-foot baby hammerhead shark, cooked and eaten over an open fire that evening. This dubious success resulted in me being acclaimed a 'real Kiwi', in an initiation ceremony that involved having the shark's blood smeared on my face.

My letters to my father mostly contained updates on my progress with swimming and questions about our family cat. The cat, a tortoiseshell with an unusually sweet temperament, had been acquired as a kitten a few months before. After a couple of regrettable incidents, I had been entrusted with a pet again. I don't recall speaking to my father on the telephone during those two months away, perhaps once, shouting tinnily at each other from opposite ends of the globe.

We visited cousins in their huge house in Herne Bay – a mansion, in my eyes, white, part-wooden, Edwardian, with a turret on the roof. My parents were married from this house, in another era, impossibly young and glamorous in photographs. Their silver wedding anniversary – marking twenty-five years together – was approaching, just as back home the Queen's Silver Jubilee was everywhere. Satisfied with the symmetry, at breakfast, the heat rising, I lazily watched while ants marched in triumph through the sweet crystals spilled from the sugar bowl.

One humid, overcast late afternoon towards the end of our stay, my mother and I caught the bus to Stanley Point, where as a girl she had often swum. As she struck out confidently to sea, leaving me on the deserted shore, fat drops of rain began to fall, soon followed by the hungry tummy rumble of thunder. My mother continued swimming as the rain advanced to a storm, waving in reassurance to where I shivered alone on the beach. When – after what seemed like decades but could only have been minutes – she emerged from the sea, I was crying. The sense of separation was acute. 'I thought you'd swim away,' I sobbed, as she dried herself briskly with a towel and promised me fish and chips. She looked surprised. 'I'll always come back,' she said.

England, when we eventually returned, seemed old and grey and tired, as did my father, who had come to meet the plane at Heathrow and drive us back to Sheffield. He had brought our winter coats with him in the car and we quickly wrapped up against the cold and damp. Dirty patches of ice and snow lay in the airport car park, listlessly, even though it was the middle of March. Two days before we had been on the beach in hot sunshine. Yet I was overjoyed to be back and eager to be reunited with the cat. Leaving her had been the hardest thing about going to New Zealand, I thought, as the car crawled up the M1, my parents strangely silent in the front.

A week after our return to Sheffield, both my father and the cat left home. Neither of them would ever come back.

At first, I didn't take in my father's unofficial departure. I was jet-lagged, disorientated and in consternation over the disappearance of the cat. At school I was the unfamiliar centre of attention – on my first day back the other girls clustered at the gate to greet me, admiring my brown legs and newly bobbed hair.

When I eventually asked where my father went at night, for he was no longer at home, my mother told me that he was working late at the bookshop. He had, somewhat controversially and unwisely as it would turn out, left his university post to join my mother in the business, and the shop had recently relocated to larger premises in Broomhill. 'Is he sleeping on the shelves?' I asked.

One evening soon after, as we sat in the living room, my mother was busy and distracted, dashing off letters one after the other. A ringing telephone took her out into the hall. I heard her exclaim 'I was just writing to you' to whoever was on the other end of the line. Inquisitive, I went to peek at the letter lying half written on the top of the pile.

I was an inveterate snooper, fearful of being left out – the scourge of being the youngest child. After we had moved into our present house, it had not taken me long to realise that the house a couple of doors along was empty. Sneaking into its garden one afternoon, my prowling was arrested by the hideous sight of a full-grown and very dead cat lying in the back yard, a yard which was to all other intents and purposes the neglected double of our own. The cat's body oozed with maggots.

Now, lifting the letter, I saw that it was addressed to a relative in New Zealand. I read the contents as if in a trance. My mother had written 'G is leaving me and the children.'

Dropping the piece of paper, I rushed to curl back up in my chair, as my mother ended her phone call and re-entered the room. I didn't say anything to her – what could I say? Once, a starling had become stuck in the chimney in the spare room of our old house in Ranmoor. We had tried to release it, but the frightened bird climbed further and further up into the dark cavity. The moment the frantic flapping ceased was even worse than the pitiful sound of invisible, agitated wings inside the chimney breast. After reading the line 'G is leaving', it felt as if that starling were trapped in my body.

Spring arrived, soft and sweet. At Easter, and for the first time, I was sent away alone, to stay with family friends in Winchester who had children around my own age. My mother telephoned often during the week I was there. She told me that she and my father were spending a few days at a place called Moreton-in-Marsh. He could not come to the phone, she said, as he had gone out for a walk, or was having a bath, or a pint in the local pub. He sent his love. A day or so after the first call, a postcard arrived in my mother's handwriting, with both of their signatures, also in my mother's handwriting, which was unusual, as generally they jointly signed birthday cards and letters. Apparently, they were still in Moreton-in-Marsh, although I noticed that, puzzlingly, the card bore a Sheffield postmark. I came to doubt the very existence of Moreton-in-Marsh, until years later, while waiting for a train at Oxford railway station, I heard the place announced on a list of destinations.

The end of April, and my tenth birthday. There was an unusual fuss about me having a party this year, which I didn't particularly want but felt unable to refuse. My father, who I hadn't seen since before my parents' alleged trip at Easter, made a brief, unexpected appearance on the day, hovering uneasily by the living-room curtains, his face in shadow. I could not make out his expression.

The following weekend, my mother took me to stay with friends in Buckinghamshire. It must have been decided that enough pretence was enough, for there, in the stuffy back room of the upstairs attic, she told me that my father was no longer going to be living with us, that he had in fact already moved in with someone else.

I allowed a tear to run down my cheek. '*I am allowing a tear to run down my cheek*', intoned the narrator in my head. That what I had realised to be true had now officially become reality did not bring relief, rather a twisting sort of desperation, an utter lack of comprehension. 'But why isn't he going to live with us?'

'Because he doesn't love me any more,' my mother answered.

Later my father telephoned. Having been evasive for so many weeks, he was suddenly eager to communicate, if only on his terms.

'Has Mummy told you?'

'Yes.'

A pause. 'Are you happy?'

'Yes.' This seemed to be the answer that was required, one that would satisfy my father, although at that moment it seemed unlikely I would ever be 'happy' again. I saw myself from above, alone in the gloom of the hall, a small figure clutching the telephone in my right hand, its receiver weeping emptiness from its mouth. At school one of the most popular games in our repertoire was 'What's the Time, Mr Wolf?'; though ostensibly to teach us counting, we fully exploited its sinister undertones. Now I sensed the wolf creeping up behind me, getting closer and closer, hot, rancid breath on my neck, sharpened claws clicking, ready to pounce. I did not turn round, still clinging to the phone, but the wolf was now inside the receiver, and I half expected the voice issuing from it to be not that of my father, but another, impatient and ravenous, announcing '*dinner time*'.

A few weeks passed. I was unwell. My head hurt, really hurt, the side of my face was swollen and painful, my throat dry, and I was so hot I wanted to rip my skin off. The doctor diagnosed mumps. The late spring was turning into summer, fresh and restless outside. Lying in my parents' bed – now my mother's bed – next to the partially open window, I could glimpse my swing, neglected in the garden. Usually I would be on it, moving back and forth manically, up, up into the lilac tree, its pale purple blossoms the colour of Parma violet sweets. Instead, I was uncomfortable and afraid. My sister, who had not had mumps, sat at a safe distance on a chair in the doorway of the room, reading to me in her low, melodious voice, from Alison Uttley's *A Traveller in Time*. The words were like cool water sliding over the stones at the bottom of a river. A river in nearby Derbyshire in fact, where the book is set, at Thackers, an old manor house belonging to the real-life Babington family, brought down by Anthony Babington's ill-fated plot to rescue the captive Mary, Queen of Scots and place her on the English throne. The book's heroine, a young girl, Penelope Taberner Cameron, flits between her present time and Elizabethan England simply by lifting the latch of a door, becoming deeply involved in the lives of the tragic Babingtons:

I looked at myself in the little mirror. My cheeks were flaming-red, my arms were sunburnt, but another sun had warmed them. The hot passions of those days flowed in my veins, I felt transfigured, old, wise, knowing a thousand things of which I had been barely conscious.

My mother washed my hot, sweaty face and hands with rose and almond-oil soap, and its rich, heady scent blurred into my sister's voice, along with images of the old, rambling manor house, where a young man strummed the tune to 'Greensleeves' on a lute, until I became part of its story, roaming its corridors in my nightgown, searching for a glass of cold water. When I was allowed to leave bed, an enormous moon face looked back at me from the dressing-table mirror.

At last, my fever dropped, the bloating in my face subsided and I returned to school. My classmates had reacted predictably to the information of my new home situation, snapping at the heels of my misery like hungry terriers. 'Your mother will have to change her name once she's not married to your father any more.' 'You won't have the same name.' 'Or live in the same house.' 'My mum said . . .'

As a result of my illness, I had been reprieved, for this term only, from my summer sports fear: the high jump. The old, cold metal bar, the stained blue mattress behind, the impossibility of the height to which we cantered one by one in our yellow aertex gym shirts and brown gym knickers. Like a reluctant and nervous horse, I would refuse to go any further.

Oblivious to the convulsions in my family, the year of official celebration marched on. At Chester Zoo, the first elephant to be born in Britain appeared in June to great fanfare and was inevitably christened Jubilee. That summer, filmmaker Derek Jarman was putting together his dystopic, anarchic movie of the same name. Released in early 1978, *Jubilee* featured an assortment of characters from Stuart Goddard (who later found fame as Adam Ant) to Toyah Willcox and punk muse Jordan. Jordan's twinsets, pink Mohican, and face boldly decorated with geometric zigzags held the film together like a giant safety pin, the symbol of punk. In the film a fictitious Elizabeth I time travels to this futuristic, lawless England to which she reacts with a mixture of disdain and dismay. Her astrologer, the infamous Dr Dee, predicts events centuries into the future, some of which would actually occur when the Conservatives gained power from Labour a couple of years later: riots, strikes, uprisings against the establishment.

My most vivid recollection of actual Jubilee celebrations is of a 'ball' – more a fancy party – that my mother attended as a last-minute addition to the guest list, going without a partner, wearing a long ice-blue dress with a high collar which beautifully offset her wavy dark hair. She had lost a lot of weight. Alongside its emotional toll, my father's departure was jeopardising both their business and our home.

The party was in Buckinghamshire, and I was to stay overnight at my gran's old house, near Baylis Park in Slough, the council house in which my father grew up, and where my aunt and cousin still lived. I was excited, because there would be prawn cocktail-flavoured crisps, Coca-Cola and sweets galore. While I was there a man I have never seen before visited. I did a double-take. He was the replica of my father, but how my father might look as a much older man. His white hair was thick, and wavy, eyes deep-set and dark. He wore a gold earring in his left ear. I was very much taken with the earring. Was he a gypsy? A pirate? The man was introduced as my grandfather, who left the family when my father, his oldest child, was thirteen. 'Who's this?' he asked my aunt. 'It's G's little girl.' He looked quizzical, patted me on the head, then dug into his trouser pocket and carefully extracted a fifty-pence piece, which he handed to me. This short, random encounter would be my sole meeting with him.

Midsummer. There was now an informal arrangement in place by which I saw my father on certain Saturdays. He didn't come into the house, but waited outside in an unfamiliar car – our own car having been taken away by bailiffs, along with various household items, as my parents' bookshop was facing bankruptcy. One designated Saturday morning, my father arrived when my mother was out. I saw that he had another person with him in the car, which was definitely not part of the agreement.

He had tried to persuade me several times to meet this person, but I had refused. Once he and this person had waited outside the school gate; I would not leave the building until they had gone. Now they had arrived at the house, my last sanctuary. I stayed where I was. My father called from a telephone box. Still I wouldn't move. Then a lot of things seemed to happen at once. My mother returned just as my father entered the house and my sister appeared in the street outside like an avenging angel, bearing down on the car and its occupant. My parents were now shouting at each other. 'I'll see my bloody daughter if I want to,' my father insisted, and his *bloody daughter* was petrified. Somewhere there was screaming, which after a while I realised came from me, and at this my parents stopped shouting. My father left the house, white-faced. As much as a year or more would pass before I saw him again. It was also the last time I would ever be in the same room as both my parents. From then on, I clung to my mother, afraid to let her out of my sight in case she might disappear, too.

The day after this episode, on the morning of Sunday 26 June, the body of a sixteen-year-old shop assistant, Jayne MacDonald, was found by children in a playground in Chapeltown, Leeds. The age and 'respectability' of the victim changed the mood – and the urgency – in the hunt for the Yorkshire serial killer, who now had his own nickname. A couple of months before, on 23 April, thirty-two-year-old Patricia Atkinson had been brutally murdered in her own flat in Bradford, but there had been no outcry in the media, more a resigned shrug, complete with tantalising speculation. The killer had also left a significant clue at the scene: a size seven boot print on a bed sheet. Like the other victims to date, Patricia, often known as Tina, had worked as a prostitute. Making an emotional appeal after Jayne died, her mother Irene MacDonald said 'How many more must die before people wake up and realise it could happen to someone they love? I feel that if [the victims] had all been Sunday school teachers, the public would have come forward with clues and the man would have been found by now.'

In August, just as we had the summer before, almost exactly the same family group as the previous year – this time *sans* my father – headed up to Scotland and the Isle of Mull. Everything was the same, just as nothing was. There was a palpable absence like an open sore. The year before, when he had been with us, the silent driver of the car we no longer had, was a blank. That summer was hot: this summer it rained constantly. We were staying with a friend whose tumbledown, tiny cottage was too small for extra guests, so we slept in an adjacent caravan. Every morning we were woken by sheep butting against the sides.

During that summer, there was a growing awareness that this was the set-up now, and we were going to have to find a way forward without my father. Sometimes the days were wretched with tension and arguments, sometimes peaceful, even beautiful. Late into the evenings my mother, rinsed out by grief and worry, wept. There was more conveyed about my father's aberrations than I perhaps needed to know. As I dropped off to sleep in the wide, pale night, she would softly recite Yeats's poem 'The Lake Isle of Innisfree'. My dreams were punctured, like an explosion of shooting stars, with its imagery: noon's purple glow and the linnet's wings of evening. We ate porridge with cream and heather honey for breakfast; watched grey seals in the water; and once, driving along a deserted road, our way was blocked by Highland cattle, resembling armed warriors from a long-forgotten clan.

That autumn a resolution was found for the bookshop, a compromise, so that the business could continue to operate. My mother remained as the manager but was no longer the owner. We were in a fugue state still. Our former house in Ranmoor came onto the market and I went with my mother to look around it, for what purpose I don't think either of us knew. I believed, momentarily, that if we were somehow able to buy back our old home – which was, in any case, unaffordable – then time would somehow be reversed. My father would put his key in the door each evening and all would be as before. I played the Abba song 'Knowing Me Knowing You' over and over again on the record player, singing mournfully and repeatedly along with the line about children and old familiar rooms, until my mother eventually requested that I turn off that particular track.

In order to remain in our home, we let out rooms to strangers. I was resistant to this, but then nothing had gone my way all year. As it happened our first two lodgers, both young women – Deborah, a shy eighteen-year-old English medical student with a permanent cold, swathed in delicate jumpers and scarves of wispy white wool, and Henriette, a warm, irrepressible secretary in her late twenties from Senegal – became an integral if temporary part of our lives, as would, to varying degrees, their successors. Henriette, in particular, was a joyous addition to home. Elegant whether in mid-length skirts and high heels or in traditional Senegalese dress, she filled her room with friends, music, flowers, fruit and cigarette smoke. She hated the cold, wet winter. In Sheffield via the British Council to learn English, she was divorced, with two small children whom she had left in the care of her mother. While Henriette was living with us, her mother died suddenly. Used to insipid British customs, and unable to articulate my own feelings about my father, I was shocked to see her express grief so openly and eloquently.

On 9 October, the body of twenty-year-old Jean Jordan was found on a disused allotment in Chorlton, south Manchester. She had been murdered eight days before. On 15 October, Jean's discarded handbag was located nearby, with a vital clue inside it – the five-pound note that her killer had given to her as payment for sex.

The year plummeted towards its end. At Christmas, I was presented with a new cat, to replace the much-lamented tortoiseshell that had mysteriously vanished the

43

same week as my father. The students who lived next door had a litter of kittens and I was allowed to choose one, pitch-black, like the cat in the book *Gobbolino, the Witch's Cat*, with green eyes like mine and a similar tendency to bad temper. She was insouciant, but she slept on the end of my bed at night, which was all I wanted.

The glass decorations on the tree twinkled painfully: little icicles of grief. I flicked at the baubles obsessively with my fingernails until they bruised. A whole year ago at Christmas I had been looking forward to the big adventure of travelling to New Zealand, which turned out to be the beginning of the upending of life. A couple of years before he left, my father had been involved in a near-fatal car crash on the motorway. His car, a pistachio-coloured Peugeot, had turned over three times with him inside it, and he had, miraculously, walked away from the accident, shaken but somehow physically unscathed. For a second he had temporarily lost concentration at the wheel. Who wouldn't reassess their life at such a moment? He was forty-seven. In my most wicked contemplations in the months after my father had gone, I would wish that he had died in that accident, because then I would understand my suffering, and, most importantly of all, he would not have left us by choice.

That Jubilee year, which had seen the unanticipated end of my parents' own quarter of a century together, had begun with a golden time which now appeared prelapsarian in contrast to the after events. I would take it out and examine it sometimes, then restore it to a safe place in memory. I have never been back to New Zealand. Superstitiously, I held fast to an omnipresent anxiety: if I did go, some as yet unforeseen catastrophe instigated by being on the other side of the world would be fully and irrevocably unleashed on my return.

Chapter Three

Don't Fear the Reaper

The sudden snow was unexpected for late March. Emerging just after midnight from the wedding reception, high up in Sheffield University's Arts Tower, reeling from a sugary surfeit of cake and sparkling wine, an impromptu celebratory snowball fight broke out in the car park. Wet white missiles fizzed through the air. A mini blizzard, quickly turning to slush in hands and underfoot, the sky above nearby Weston Park still ominously heavy with it.

It was a year since my father had departed our family, and my sister had just got married.

My sister's wedding was the first major family occasion without my father present; he had decamped for good. From then on, he would appear as little more than an outline in any official capacity.

The sky looked as solid as a throat lozenge. Drifting not too far in my thoughts, I came to land in recent memory, inside the museum in the park itself. There, I had stood many times holding tightly to my father's hand as we gazed up at my favourite resident: the stuffed polar bear. Off-white fur, yellowish with age, ghastly teeth. I both loved and feared that bear. It seemed so alone, away from its Arctic home, and yet, veiled in shadowy lighting, I was terrified that it would jump down and embrace me between its jaws at any moment. We always spoke in whispers around it.

Past the museum, and the statue of Ebenezer Elliott, the radical 'Corn Law Rhymer', was Crookes Valley Park, its benign boating lake the scene of a crime a few summers before. The crime had been committed by me. My father crouched by the water in a white shirt with the sleeves rolled up, smiling broadly, as I ran towards him. Throwing myself into his arms, I somehow knocked his brand-new sunglasses out of his hand and into the middle of the lake. We watched helplessly as they sank beneath the surface and were swallowed up. My father's face was inscrutable.

The moment, the sunlit summer afternoon, which had been perfect, was ruined. I was six, and this was my first experience of disappointing my father; it would not be my last. Were the sunglasses still there, at the bottom of the lake, waiting to be recovered, I wondered, shivering now, as the wedding party piled into cars and taxis. If they were retrieved would time go backwards, and bring my father with it? Such were the melodramatic bargaining discussions I had with myself.

When I tried to picture my father these days, he was always wearing sunglasses. I could never make out his eyes.

As it turned out, my internal soliloquies about his imagined return were futile. Several months after my sister's wedding, on a scorching campsite in the south of France, my mother informed me that she and my father were now divorced. I hadn't seen him since the previous summer; he had moved away from Sheffield.

Will you change your name back, then? I asked. She looked puzzled. No. Will they have children? A pause. No. *She doesn't like children.*

I behaved very badly for the next few days and even claimed that I almost drowned in the swimming pool while my mother was reading on a sun lounger and *not paying attention.* The water was so blue, so inviting, away from the crowds and the heat. I could slide slowly to the bottom like the sunglasses in the lake, and never emerge. No one would notice. The Blue Öyster Cult's '(Don't Fear) The Reaper', the hit of the summer, blared out from a transistor radio someone had placed near the edge of the pool. But the survival instinct was stronger than any morbid death wish. I fought my way, spluttering and indignant, to the surface.

No one had noticed, in fact.

We were staying for a month, in a static caravan owned by some generous friends. The campsite was quiet and shady, covered in pine trees, the earth sandy. The pine-cones were warm and aromatic, evocative of a different holiday in the before times.

My mother didn't drive and in any case we had no car, so the journey from Sheffield had been made with another single-parent family. The father, also newly separated, had a daughter about to turn eleven, just like me. Molly and I had hit it off immediately, unusually: she was forthright, fun, and adventurous whereas I hung back cautiously.

We had taped the Top 40 from our local station, Radio Hallam, before leaving, and forced our parents to play it continuously in the car during the long days of the journey from South Yorkshire to the Mediterranean. It was mesmerisingly hot. Molly and I smeared our mouths with sickly sweet, cherry-flavoured lip gloss which came free with *Mates* magazine, and sucked on Opal Fruits and Spangles till our tummies hurt.

Once in France, during one late afternoon, Molly and I were supposedly resting in the small guesthouse at which we'd stopped for the night. The heavy wooden shutters were closed against the heat, and we lay on the bed in nothing but our knickers. Molly suggested we 'practise kissing', only for my mother to walk in just as we were experimentally pressing our sweaty flat chests together. She said nothing except that tea was ready. I was embarrassed; Molly found it hilarious.

The destination reached, our two families separated: we to our pine-shaded campsite, Molly and her father to a bigger one a few miles away, complete with adventure playground and swimming pools. My mother and I were collected each day like elderly relatives and driven back to our secluded mobile home at night, when the fireflies were out and the cicadas clicking. Other Sheffield families had descended on the big campsite, adults and children looking slightly bewildered, askance. Quite a few recon-figurations were under way, with new relationships and different set-ups emerging, playing out like a tableau in front of my avid eyes.

In the somnolent, baking afternoons by the pool or at the beach, the adults drank rosé, Cinzano, and pastis, smoked cigarettes ruthlessly, and rubbed Ambre Solaire tanning oil into each other's crisply burning bodies. I picked up the women's damp, discarded Jilly Cooper books with their soft-focus covers and enticing girls' names: *Harriet, Octavia*. My mother, the only adult not part of an obvious couple, was somewhat detached from this melee, reading *The Golden Notebook*, and not enjoying it. She moved on to an Edna O'Brien novel, the title of which declared that *August Is a Wicked Month*.

The children were left to their own devices. Our own devices. Molly was in her element, I was not, acutely self-conscious in my first so-called 'bikini' – a modest two-piece. Molly flaunted her much skimpier one, which had string ties, like a fashion model's. She made friends quickly and eagerly. I hung back shyly. Molly's honey-coloured skin tanned easily. My mushroom-white skin did not.

Within days, I was sunburnt to the point of shivery sickness, and my mother and I retreated to spend time alone. In the cool dimness of our caravan, she assiduously applied stinking pink calamine lotion from a bottle onto my sore shoulders and dissolved a Junior Disprin in water. To take my mind off the sunburn, I read Rumer Godden's bitter coming-of-age novel *The Greengage Summer*, captivated by its picture of an eccentric, impoverished English family thrown into chaos while on holiday in 1920s France. Sensual and sinister, the book is narrated by Cecil, a girl of thirteen. Their widowed mother hospitalised, Cecil and her assorted siblings are left to run wild in their hotel and the surrounding countryside, under the dubious protection of a mysterious stranger. Between Cecil and her older sister Joss there is much talk of something called 'the curse'. When Cecil experiences 'the curse' herself for the first time, she is congratulated on becoming 'a woman . . . ready for love'.

I interrogated my mother intently about this 'curse'. Was it a bad spell? Was love a curse? From what I'd seen of it so far it must be. As she began to explain about periods – most unwelcome information – my cheeks grew hot on top of the sunburn. Is this what becoming 'a woman' meant? It was part of it, replied my mother. Just a part of growing up, she added, reassuringly.

Well, it won't happen to *me*, I muttered, rebelliously. I'll emigrate.

By the time we returned to the big campsite, sunburn in abeyance, Molly had definitively absconded from our friendship. She clattered and chattered around with the older girls in the group, who had made a pet of her, lip-syncing to Blondie, wearing heart-shaped plastic sunglasses and revealing tops. For her birthday an ice-cream cake stuck all over with sparklers was produced, and Molly almost fainted with excitement. I watched balefully across the shimmering expanse of the swimming pool, and cried bitterly to my mother that evening, when we were alone in our caravan. She attempted to soothe me. People could have more than one friend, possessiveness wasn't healthy, and my feelings would pass. Her words went over my head. I want to go home, I screamed. I want . . . The 'D' word hovered between us in the claustrophobic August air. I didn't say the rest. An image of my father, comforting portly stomach straining against his old gardening jumper with the leather patches sewn onto the elbows, flickered into my mind and was just as quickly snuffed out.

The three-day car journey back to Sheffield was insufferable. Molly and I did not speak: our only communication was to silently and viciously pinch and push if either one encroached on an inch of the other's territory in the cramped back seat. The adults in the front of the car were silent too, undoubtedly fed up with their warring respective children. All they'd wanted was a break in the sun with congenial company. We were dropped off back at our house on a rainy afternoon near the end of August. It was several years before we would see Molly and her family again.

Although in social terms the holiday had been a minor disaster, it had conclusively drawn a line under childhood. The knowledge that my father and mother were now legally severed for good, the imminent move from junior to senior school, and most of all the rather louche summer-soaked glimpse into the world of adults – even if their version of adulthood wasn't one to which I necessarily wanted to belong – all ensured that, like Cecil in *The Greengage Summer*, certain things were now behind me.

On our return, the papers brimmed with the disappearance of a schoolgirl in rural Devon. Out on her bicycle, delivering local newspapers on the afternoon of Saturday 19 August, thirteen-year-old Genette Tate had paused to chat with two friends before cycling ahead of them up a quiet country lane. When the other girls caught up with her a few minutes later, they found her bicycle lying on its side in the middle of the road, with newspapers scattered around. Genette was never found, and after several months her image faded from view, as the media circus moved on, to be renewed with fresh appeals on anniversaries as the years and then the decades passed.

The image of Genette's abandoned bicycle, one wheel still spinning, is indelible in my memory. The last time her father had seen her, on that warm summer afternoon, she had been 'doing her puzzle book' in the garden. All of us girls who, like Genette in 1978, had some limited but increasing degree of independence, who also rode bicycles, did puzzle books, caught buses on our own and played in the woods, skimming stones across brooks and streams, watched dragonflies hover, walked to school, to the local shops with coins from our mothers snug in our hands and a shopping list memorised in our heads, and who dodged, somehow, the footsteps behind us, the lurking transit van, the man 'interfering with himself' on the path ahead – all of us who persisted into adulthood and middle age and beyond – our survival seems to me haphazard. The colliding with evil, that malignant dark star forever on our horizon, was always a mere spasm away: not preordained in life's great lottery, but random, and terrible, terrible luck.

Against this uneasy backdrop I continued my journey into adolescence. In September, secondary school and The Vosene Years began. Dandruff was my worst fear. Vosene's addictive, druggy aroma accompanied the long baths I took on Thursday evenings in the hour after hockey practice and before *Top of the Pops*. Lying under the full glare of electric light, I transformed the bath rack into my personal tray, like an old-fashioned film star from a 1940s movie reclining in a sumptuous bed. A hot flannel coyly arranged across the two promising bumps newly swelling on my chest, I surveyed my treasures: a plate of toast and peanut butter, a mug of milky tea and the latest issue of *Smash Hits*, *My Guy* or *Photolove* – the last two purchased without my mother's knowledge. The cloudy water would be illicitly perfumed with her for-special-occasions-only Badedas foaming oil. 'Things happen after a Badedas bath,' the adverts threatened.

The raw, muddy afternoon spent on the hockey pitch at the appropriately named Coldwell Lane in Crosspool would slowly be soaked away. While most of the other girls were collected in cars after practice, I would usually wait for the bus. By late October the dark drew itself down suddenly like a blind, and I felt conspicuous if I were at the bus stop alone. More than once, a car, a crepuscular creature slithering out of nowhere, approached and slowed, the driver's window winding down. In the light remaining I could barely make out who or what was inside. 'No thank you,' I would say, when the inevitable lift was offered, before adding an untruth: 'I'm waiting for my father to collect me. He'll be along soon.'

In a few short months of secondary school my cohort had undergone an irreversible metamorphosis. No longer obediently collecting milk-bottle tops for the Blue Peter Appeal, unevenly and inexpertly playing the recorder in Friday assembly before listening to the classical record of the week, those same girls were now gyrating suggestively on top of their desks before afternoon registration, uniform kilts hiked up, shouting in loud unison the chorus to John Travolta's 'Greased Lightnin''. We all knew the lyrics had been changed for radio play from 'the chicks will cream' to 'the chicks will scream' although none of us knew what 'cream' in this context actually meant.

I watched this spectacle admiringly but did not participate. Despite my longing to grow up, I was still semi-cocooned in childhood, and specifically its books: the beloved time-slip novels *When Marnie Was There*, *Charlotte Sometimes*, *Tom's Midnight Garden* and *Come Back, Lucy* – all of which had characters with, unlike me, the convenient ability to step into and sometimes even alter the outcomes of the past. *A Little Princess*, whose protagonist Sara Crewe was a lavishly loved child until her father died, leaving her a penniless orphan in the school where she had been the star pupil, and *The Railway Children*, with another absent father, culminating in Bobbie's anguished cry of 'Daddy, my daddy!', were acutely painful for me to read.

At school, our abilities, or lack of them, were very much on display. Classes were split into 'divisions' for certain subjects. One of the teachers, who seemed to have been reluctantly resurrected from another century, controlled the lower division – for which I had automatically qualified – with alternating, unnerving childlike sweetness and unpredictable rages. According to her, I was 'stupid' and on repeated occasions the chalky blackboard rubber was hurled explicitly in my direction. Despite my lack of prowess in any sport, after the first attack I managed to duck every time.

I remember little about our school excursions, apart from one Classics trip to Fishbourne in Sussex. Adam and the Ants were at the top of the charts: one classmate's mother had sat up all night embroidering 'Ant Music for Sex People' on her otherwise mild-mannered daughter's silk bomber jacket, just for the occasion. The furore that caused was more memorable than any Roman mosaics.

Differences other than those of academic or sporting ability were becoming more apparent. A few of us were or had been on bursaries to help pay the fees; we recognised and tacitly ignored each other at the second-hand uniform shop; we sat together with our packed lunches because the cooked school dinners were too expensive; we did not go on skiing trips. I was agonisingly aware that everyone knew my mother let out rooms in our house to strangers, sometimes – the horror – to people from other countries. There was a world of ignorance and prejudice of which I was just beginning to be fully aware. One of our lodgers at this time, a distinguished professor of engineering who was teaching for a term at the university, was Japanese. He had a daughter about my age back home, and often walked me to school, carrying my hockey stick, endlessly polite and charming. He was clearly bothered by the absence of my own father, although he never mentioned this to me. As we got closer to the school I would make excuses; there really was no need for him to walk me all the way up to the gate. This was because the first time he did so someone had audibly muttered the word 'Jap'.

Away from school, our bookshop became my refuge, and catered for much of the education that my teachers did not provide. Having improbably survived my parents' divorce, it remained at the centre of family life. Before I was twelve – the age at which I was given my own back-door key – I would regularly trudge up Newbould Lane towards Broomhill after school. If my mother was on her own there I would boil the kettle in the cramped back area to make her a cup of tea, and munch a treat of a Mr Kipling Cherry Bakewell from a packet under the till. I was allowed to tenderly place book purchases into orange-coloured paper bags stamped with the Penguin logo, sealing them with Sellotape from the dispenser before handing them over to a customer in the manner of a host body relinquishing its demon. While my mother cashed up I ran up and down the stairs to call 'Sorry, we're closed' in the direction of any remaining customers. I approached the top floor with caution at that time of day, especially when the evenings got darker. Anyone could be up there, waiting in those dim, expectant rooms.

The bookshop had become the go-to place for writers visiting Sheffield: it hosted literary events featuring contemporary authors. William Trevor spent the majority of his visit with his trouser zip at half-mast, spotted only when the photo galleys came through from the *Sheffield Telegraph*. I sat, cross-legged on the floor in the shadowy topmost room of the shop, as a packed audience listened to a long-haired, bearded Tom Paulin read softly, almost inaudibly, from his debut poetry collection, *A State of Justice*.

By the time I was fourteen I had started helping out on Saturdays to earn pocket money – most of which was spent on black lace fingerless gloves, records, make-up and the endless concoctions I would uselessly apply to my spotty skin in the hope of calming it into submission. By this time, the regular customers included Phil Oakey, lead singer of Sheffield's coolest synth band, The Human League. Hanging around the till, I would be rewarded with a close appreciation of Oakey's famous asymmetrical haircut, having seen it through the TV screen earlier that week on *Top of the Pops*. But the task I liked best – once I had worked through my first, hated, chore, breaking up and flattening the mountain of boxes which the stock arrived in – was unpacking and shelving the brand-new books. In this way I read and absorbed so much – the green-backed Virago Modern Classics – Angela Carter, Rosamond Lehmann, Antonia White, F. Tennyson Jesse,

Elizabeth Taylor – and the Women's Press titles which featured more diverse and more obviously feminist literature – Toni Cade Bambara, Toni Morrison, Alice Walker, Michèle Roberts. I imbibed other books too, secretly, in horror and fascination. Kathy Acker's *Blood and Guts in High School* made a curious companion to Vincent Bugliosi and Curt Gentry's *Helter Skelter: The True Story of the Manson Murders*, shoved underneath my bed alongside forgotten plates of congealed cheese on toast, where no one would see. Its uneasy equilibrium was one Acker herself might have understood. This interest in violence – if it could be quantified as interest – was an attempt to gain some control over fear, but that control, like the violence, was amorphous and slippery.

We all saw the papers, watched the news on TV and heard the radio. Each year that we grew older and left childhood further behind, the man we all referred to by that unforgettable epithet stole more women's and girls' lives away. We were eleven, then twelve, then thirteen. In these years, the years I did not see my father, it was as if he had been replaced by a shadow figure, one that was menacing and faceless.

When Jayne MacDonald, the youngest murder victim, had been killed in 1977, any one of us could have been one of the children who discovered her body: in a few years we would be Jayne's age. We were growing up fast, whether we wanted to or not. In January 1978 twenty-one-year-old Yvonne Pearson was killed in Bradford and eighteen-year-old Helen Rytka in Huddersfield. Early

April 1979 saw the murder of nineteen-year-old build-ing society clerk Josephine Whitaker in Halifax. On 1 September, twenty-year-old Bradford University student Barbara Leach became the next victim. The killer of these young women in Leeds, Bradford, Halifax, Huddersfield, Wakefield and Manchester remained, as the police and the media put it, 'at large'.

By this time, in Sheffield and other northern cities, recession bit hard, to paraphrase the first line of Joy Divi-sion's 'Love Will Tear Us Apart', and everything closed down, as The Specials' haunting, restless 1981 Number 1 song 'Ghost Town' emphasised – it could have been Sheffield they were driving through in the accompanying video, too wary to get out of the car. Britain was in limbo; one government had gone out and in the late spring of 1979, another would come in.

A few days earlier, after my twelfth birthday party in our garden, the swing had been dismantled; I was deemed too old for it. Before this rite of passage I posed ironically for birthday photographs, my hair long with its inevitable middle parting. Within the year I would have had it all cut off, and grown several inches taller, both of which seemed acts of defiance. I put away my treasured hair slides, gleaming with their childish silver stars, gold hearts and enamelled ladybirds.

New experiences and desires began to surface. One of these was music. The first 45-inch single I ever bought for myself was the Boomtown Rats' 'Rat Trap'; the album, Blondie's *Parallel Lines*. And although determined on the path of gloom, I loved the exuberance of disco. Kate Bush took care of my more expressive instincts, but my absolute ideal was Patti Smith. Her carefully curated and superbly androgynous image, the unshaved legs and armpits casually yet magnificently displayed, the harsh and discordant voice, frantic, incomprehensible and often dirge-like lyrics – all were manna to ears and eyes sick already of the prettifying and packaging that seemed to be expected of teenage girls. I stopped applying Immac to my still-hairless legs and a well-thumbed copy of Smith's stream-of-consciousness book *Babel* joined Kathy Acker and the Manson Family underneath my bed.

Politics was a topic that had always been freely discussed at home, yet I observed that groupthink dominated the world immured within the battlemented walls of school. History was one of the few subjects in which I had not been relegated to a lower-ranking division, but I would later lose interest in it following the Rule Britannia mania which seemed to automatically go along with the Falklands War. In any case, I had learned my lesson when I asked a question about the hunger strikers in the Maze Prison. Convicted IRA paramilitaries, the 'blanket men', were refused political prisoner status by the British government. Bobby Sands died in May 1981: we were never officially taught the background to The Troubles. The history teacher's response to my 'impertinence' was one of glassy-eyed fury.

Prior to this, the winter of 1978–79 – the third coldest of the twentieth century – had unexpectedly granted me one of my first real school friends, a friendship that would inadvertently help me navigate the mysteries of sex. Verity lived in a tall Gothic Victorian house with two narrow glass slits either side of the attic windows. She had an air of sophistication and confidence which I did not possess. She called her parents by their first names. I had tried this only once with my mother, who pretended not to hear.

When I stayed the night during that long, snowy winter, Verity and I often slept in an attic room, dunking chocolate flakes into our hot milk, discussing the contents of the 'men's magazines' we'd discovered stashed in a corner of one of the damp, spidery cellars in my own house, left behind by an unidentified previous occupant. The images had made me feel woozy in a way I didn't understand. I'd also seen, at another house, a casual screening of the film *Emmanuelle* – which was definitely something I didn't mention at home.

Watching over us in the attic was the large skull of a ram which was kept hung on a hook behind the door. The lurid photographs remembered from *Fiesta*, *Knave* and *Mayfair*, the strange sensations they brought forth, remain connected with that cold, polished skull, its curved horns seeming never less than alive, the empty sockets boring into my own fascinated eyes. We named the skull 'God' in the belief that it was all-seeing. Before we went to sleep, huddled together in one bed against the cold, we would drape a scarf over God. I slept on the side nearest the door, waking intermittently through the night, in case the scarf slipped off to reveal the cleaned white bone blazing like a lonely, ancient moon, the pitiless black hollows on either side.

My longing to be outside childhood, to enter the adult world, came and went. School bitched along with unceasing regularity. My sister and brother-in-law belonged to a local amateur dramatic society; as I got older I would help out with front-of-house activities such as selling programmes. One production was of Peter Nichols's 1974 play *Chez Nous* – an already dated study of middle-class English shenanigans in France. The couples acting in the play were all friends off-stage; by the end of the run it was obvious that one of the fictional couples was having an affair in real life, which certainly enlivened a very dull if slightly risqué drama. I had a part in *Chez Nous* in an entirely meta-fictional way. The teenage daughter of one of the couples becomes pregnant by the husband of the other couple; she never appears in the play but is depicted through slides on a projector. I'd been camping with my sister and brother-in-law the summer before the play's run; it was my averted face and demure pinafore dress shown in the accompanying slides; watching this moment on stage was perturbing and yet transfixing. I was seeing myself as an alternative persona, another possibility, a character in a story. Who would I choose to be? As my body changed, I felt the first awareness of how others might now view me differently.

At the party after the final production, flushed with imagined sophistication, feeling very grown-up for almost fourteen, I wore my new dress from Bringing it All Back

Home, on West Street – one of several Sheffield shops named after Bob Dylan albums. The dress was a long, block-patterned batik, with a low-cut dark blue yoke at the neck. It glittered all over with tiny mirrors which caught the light when I moved, and so I moved often. 'Soon you'll be able to have any man you want,' a much older man informed me, after admiring the dress, and staring for too long at the neckline. He imparted this information under breath that was uncomfortably close and which reeked of too much wine. I didn't wear the dress again.

I was learning that threats did not always come from strangers, and dangers might not be immediately obvious.

The hunt for Yorkshire's serial killer accelerated as winter began in earnest that year. Despite the substantial, biting fear in the air, as reliable now as early morning frost, I still went out stubbornly on my bicycle, cycling my streets, from Hunter's Bar to Ecclesall, up Cemetery Road to Kenwood, bumping over tree roots so old and deep they spilt the pavements. Down Sharrow Vale, across Endcliffe Park and on to its adjoining park, Bingham. Pushing the bike up the steep track, I entered the solitude of Whiteley Woods, trusting to the lonely path as the trees closed around me.

Chapter Four

Winter Kills

Friday, 2 January 1981, the last day of the Christmas holidays, was cold and drizzly in Sheffield. There was, however reluctantly, a possibility of taking a walk that day. My head hurt from being cooped up indoors, reading my school books – *Jane Eyre* and *Julius Caesar* – on a manic loop: gothic imagination fused with ancient Roman law. Late in the morning, sundry family members, along with visitors from overseas who'd been staying for New Year, descended on Haworth, just over an hour's drive away. At the Brontë Parsonage Museum I saw for the first time the dresses, gloves and shoes that had belonged to Charlotte, Emily, and Anne, displayed in their glass cases, and marvelled at how grown women could be so tiny. Encased too were the preserved miniature books containing the tales of Gondal and Angria that the sisters had dreamt up with their brother Branwell to while away the intense, interminable hours of childhood, stories they would become obsessed with, inspired – and, in some indefinable way – ruined by.

I was shocked and morbidly impressed by the immediacy of the churchyard. I had not expected it to be so oppressively close to the house; the long, doleful slabs of its tombstones the only view from the front-facing, obstinately small square windows; the shadow of the moors looming suddenly up at the back. It was growing dark and beginning to snow as we left Haworth to drive home to Sheffield across those same moors. I remember all of this clearly – almost forensically – because of what would happen next.

The following Monday, 5 January, was to be the start of the new term, but, as it turned out, my school was unexpectedly closed. A man had been arrested that Friday night, after we made our way back to the city through the silence of the midwinter darkness. At 4 p.m., around the same time we were departing Haworth, the man had left his home in nearby Bradford to drive, first to Leeds, then on to Sheffield. By 10 p.m., when I was getting ready for bed, his car, a brown Rover with stolen number plates attached with black tape, was cruising the red-light district around Broomhall: just around the corner from incongruously large, beatifically beautiful Victorian villas. The man picked up a young woman soliciting on Havelock Square, and drove with her to nearby Melbourne Avenue, the quiet tree-lined cul-de-sac directly behind my school, a complex of gloomily imposing Victorian buildings and playing fields. They agreed on a fee of ten pounds for sex with a condom, but after ten minutes gave up as the man was unable to sustain an erection. At 10:30 p.m. the headlights of a police car on patrol abruptly illuminated the two people inside the Rover. Three evenings later the

68

whole world would know the man's identity: Peter William Sutcliffe, the so-called 'Yorkshire Ripper', the serial killer who had, since 1975, attacked and murdered women across the region – mostly in the towns and cities of West Yorkshire, not far from the Brontës' Haworth – Halifax, Bradford, Wakefield, Leeds. Sheffield, the largest city in the extreme south of the county, was simply the next stop in a sick tour of terror.

In a sense, we had been waiting for the Ripper to visit for months, even years.

By early 1978 – three years before our January trip to Haworth – West Yorkshire police's ongoing investigation had reached breaking point. Then, in March, a letter arrived at headquarters addressed to George Oldfield, the assistant chief constable heading the inquiry. Over the course of the next year and three months, two more letters were sent, signed 'Jack the Ripper', and, most significantly, a tape, all purporting to be from the killer. The police changed course and, without any concrete evidence that this was not a hoax, focused on Sunderland, from where the communications originated.

In late June of 1979, the recording of 'Wearside Jack', his soft, wheedling voice taunting the beleaguered Oldfield, was broadcast over and over again, on buses, in shopping centres, in university halls. It played over the airwaves of our local radio station in Sheffield like a twisted nightly entertainment. 'I'm Jack. I see you are still having no luck catching me. I have the greatest respect for you, George, but Lord! You are no nearer catching me now than four years ago when I started. I reckon your boys are letting you down, George. They can't be much good, can they?' I was more used to taping the Top 40 than listening to recordings of supposed killers. From my bedroom window I would stare, transfixed, into the blackness of our back garden, imagining that 'he' was somewhere out there in the darkness.

My earliest memory of the case – and a visual image that perseveres to this day – is of a group of men – they are always men – standing over the motionless figure of a woman, lying dead on the ground, on wasteland, parkland, a children's playground. Most of the injuries inflicted on the Ripper's victims were implemented with routine domestic tools such as hammers and screwdrivers – frenzied, brutal attacks that would leave one survivor requiring over fifty stitches in the back of her head – and were too horrific to be detailed in full until the trial. But everyone, even children, could guess from where the 'Yorkshire Ripper' sobriquet came. Its origin was Jack the Ripper, the unidentified man who had murdered at least five women, some working as prostitutes, in the Whitechapel area of London's East End in the late summer of 1888. He had been the bogeyman of myth for nearly a century. The press had soon dubbed this latest serial killer with the Ripper moniker, and both the media and the police often referred to him with something close to affection even as the case became more drawn out, baffling and terrifying. 'Our friend', 'the lad', or 'chummy'

– their cheerful linguistic diminishing of the killer – even as he was simultaneously built up into a monster familiar from horror or folklore – was made in public and to newspaper and television reporters, who printed verbatim what the police told them.

Depending on their reputation or profession, the women who were murdered were categorised as either 'innocents' or 'good-time girls' at best, 'whores' at worst; never mind that they were all mothers, wives, sisters, daughters. Working-class women, living in inner-city poverty, almost overwhelmingly single parents, who worked the streets to provide for their children, were treated with contempt, arrested and fined so that their only option was to go back on the streets again. A total of twenty-six children lost their mothers at the hands of Sutcliffe.

In October 1979, Jim Hobson, a senior detective on the case, made a direct appeal to the Ripper at a press conference:

> [He] has made it clear that he hates prostitutes. Many people do. We, as a police force, will continue to arrest prostitutes. But the Ripper is now killing innocent girls. That indicates your mental state and that you are in urgent need of medical attention. You have made your point. Give yourself up before another innocent woman dies.

Growing up in this atmosphere, with a body that was changing and a sexuality that was burgeoning, was confusing and challenging. The messages I received were decidedly mixed.

In pop culture, Debbie Harry, confident and sexy in figure-hugging electric blue and sunshine yellow, Poly Styrene in her baggy clothes, Chrissie Hynde, Siouxsie Sioux, and The Slits all appeared to me to be strong, independent women. I loved their music, wishing I were older and able to go to their gigs, or to understand the references in my brother's weekly edition of the *New Musical Express*. They appeared – superficially, at least – worlds away and yet somehow connected to the women who campaigned against *The Sun* newspaper's infamous Page 3 and who were characterised by large parts of society and the media as joyless 'libbers'.

But most of the bands I watched on *Top of the Pops* were fronted by men with a couple of young women in tight pencil skirts miming the backing vocals. The election of Margaret Thatcher as the UK's first female prime minister, after the Conservative victory in May 1979, was hardly trailblazing for the UK's female population in general.

And whether I liked it or not, my body was catching up. A packet of Kotex sanitary pads – given to me by my mother not long after our holiday in France in 1978 – was stuffed at the back of my underwear drawer. For over two years, unrequired, they gathered dust. The morning of my first period was a Saturday in October 1980; I was due to meet up with my father. Our contact had finally been resumed following a court order, after two years of me refusing to see him. Because I had been instructed not to discuss routine bodily functions with men, I suffered through the day, saying I was tired and had a headache when he showed concern over my paleness. I had already grasped that periods were a furtive and shameful occurrence, but an essential part of growing up, just like the training bra – training for what, exactly – I had been bought a year before. Teased at school for being virtually flat-chested and still wearing a vest, I demanded that my mother take me to Marks & Spencer on Fargate. There the sales assistant produced a tiny white item. My disappointment showed, as I had hoped for something black and lacy. 'I wanted something more . . . alluring,' I tried to explain, except I had only seen the word written down and pronounced it 'allering'.

Things came unstuck when my period – I had only been having them for a few months – began unexpectedly at school half-term, while I was away on my own, staying with friends near Cambridge. Not yet accustomed to my monthly appointment I had brought nothing with me. I told no one and for the first day made a panicky rudimentary pad out of toilet paper. The next day, I was, together with the oldest boy of the family – with whom I had been in excited correspondence since they had come to stay with us at New Year – dropped off in Cambridge city centre for a few hours. Here was my chance. 'I just need to get something from Boots,' I said, casually. He waited outside as I grabbed a pack of sanitary pads, paid, and asked for a large carrier bag, which, although the day was freezing, I topped off with my scarf to hide the evidence. I then went to the toilets in the public library. When I came out I was smiling with achievement. He smiled back and took my hand as we walked in the early spring sunshine across Parker's Piece. *A boy is holding my hand.* I could hardly breathe for happiness.

The rest of the week was a masterclass of deception. 'No, it's OK, I don't want to go swimming, thank you.' 'No, really.' There was no waste bin in the bathroom of the house. Once again mortification had taken over: I could not easily access the bin in the kitchen, so I wrapped up the used sanitary pads and hid them in my small rucksack. When I arrived back home in Sheffield at the end of the week after a long coach journey, I finally disposed of the acrid-smelling, bloodstained evidence.

As the Ripper attacks and murders increased, there was a paralysing atmosphere of fear, alongside pockets of defiance. The killer had targeted women working as prostitutes because they were vulnerable and would be more willing to get into his car, more easily persuaded to go to remote areas where they would be killed and dumped. Yet Sutcliffe murdered students, bank clerks, shop assistants, as well as sex workers. The repeated assertion that the Ripper was on a mission to rid the North of streetwalkers would later be used as a line of defence by Sutcliffe himself at his trial.

On 20 August 1980, forty-seven-year-old civil servant Marguerite Walls was killed in Leeds. She was walking home after working late into the evening to make up the time before her summer holiday.

In November 1980, Sutcliffe murdered Jacqueline Hill, a twenty-year-old Leeds University student studying English. She was followed and struck down as she got off the evening bus to make the short walk to her halls of residence. From then on, I was no longer allowed to walk home alone from school. The fear of where the Ripper would strike next was tangible. It seemed to permeate everything, dank, mossy and slimy as Frog Walk, running alongside the high walls of the General Cemetery. It slid, cold and viscous, into my dreams at night, like the mercury escaping from a thermometer.

Every second Saturday during that time, I would, despite what I had been warned against, get into a stranger's car. The difference was that the stranger was my father – known, and semi-known, just as his simultaneous presence and absence continued to pervade our house. Schrodinger's Dad, half dead, half alive.

Wherever he had gone, it would appear that my father did not need anything from his former life, including his children. His books still filled the bookshelves; his records – Frank Sinatra, Charles Aznavour, Diana Ross, Glen Campbell, Shirley Bassey – were stacked by the record player. The house contained everything that he and my mother had assembled together and carried back and forth across the globe from New Zealand to England and back twice again: their 1950s wedding china that we still used every day, the dining-room set with the rosewood table and matching chairs, the paintings on the walls that as a couple they had selected. The green leather Scandinavian 1960s tulip chair in which, as a very small child, I used to spin around until I was dizzy, is today dilapidated, sitting like a rebuke from the past in the corner of my own living room.

My misery during these 'access visits' was profound. My father would soon give up the veneer of small talk, and when he wasn't goading me with questions such as 'What do your friends think about you coming from a broken home?' he would rage at my mother and invariably anyone else I dared to mention, plead with me to come and visit him and his new wife whom I continued to refuse to meet, or, as often as not, simply cry, so that I would end up comforting him over my own stubborn implacability. I would throw up before every meeting, and sometimes afterwards, too.

Looking back now, I feel desperately sorry for my father. He had changed his life, why couldn't I accept it? But I didn't want to. At home, my mother either berated him or extolled the man he had been. I never really knew who he was at all. I certainly could never tell him anything about myself. If, for whatever reason, I wasn't getting on with my mother, who was heartbroken and under huge stress, I was afraid that my father would take me away from her.

My mother and I were especially close, and although this could be punctuated with arguments and silences, they never lasted long. She was my protector and I felt fiercely protective of her too, even when I was behaving, as I often did, in a less than ideal daughter-like fashion. This fierceness extended to any potential partners who might hover into view, as well as, admittedly, feelings of possessiveness about her having the opportunity to focus on someone other than me. One evening, a less than suitable suitor rang the front doorbell. I answered, suspiciously. 'I've come to take your mother out to dinner,' the man announced, with a hesitant smile. 'She's already eaten,' I retorted, and slammed the door in his face.

When my parents' marriage broke up, the girls in my class had formed a circle around me – not a circle to shield me, but one of suspicion and taunting. I was the first girl in my year whose parents got divorced. Somehow, in the very early days of my parents' separation, my 'friends' knew before I did that my father was living just round the corner from our school, on the same road, in fact, with his new partner.

My mother went round there one evening and broke a window.

1980 had been a bad year, even without the Ripper. Early on, several classmates had discovered some limericks I'd written about them, and when they removed the offending articles from my desk to confront me by means of an impromptu kangaroo court in the school library they saw fit to replace them with a selection of dead birds, nestled within the old Victorian desk. It was decreed that I would be sent 'to Coventry', that is, not spoken to by anyone – for an entire year. I don't recall any teacher intervening in this incident (pastoral care was non-existent) and I certainly never relayed it to my family. Perhaps I thought I deserved it. Two of the subjects of the limericks were actual friends and for that I deeply regretted my actions, as well as the taboo subjects I'd also written about, reflecting a few of my current preoccupations – menstruation (this was the autumn of my first period) and masturbation.

I cultivated certain methods with which to deal with the swirling sadness that weighed me down. One was to play truant from school. Unlike today, where there are myriad insidious means of bullying via social media, the nastiness began and ended at the school gates. Out of school, I was safe. At least, I thought I was.

It is actually far easier, as a child, to disappear on a temporary basis, than as an adult. There is the automatic assumption that you are being supervised somewhere else. I knew that I could have a day away without being checked up on, as long as a note from my mother appeared with me at school the next morning to explain my absence. I had secreted a few of these notes, rather than giving them to the school secretary, as was the rule. Neatly written on pale blue Basildon Bond notepaper in my mother's cursive handwriting, it was easy to change the date on an old note. There was always the chance that the headmistress would call her at work, but this usually only happened if she wanted to make a threat about the non-payment of school fees, which my father had ceased contributing to, just as he had stopped paying any maintenance.

On these mornings of illicit freedom I would leave the house via the front door as usual after breakfast, and instead of going out of the gate, would turn up the path which ran along the side of the house, concealed from those inside. I would wait there until my mother left for work. Then I would let myself in through the back door with my key, run upstairs to my bedroom, change out of school uniform, smear frosted eyeshadow over my eyelids, apply mascara (either purple or green; I considered myself to be post-punk) to my lashes and complete the disguise with blusher and lip gloss. I was getting tall; I could almost pass for fourteen or fifteen or even sixteen, surely legitimate ages to be off school? I would leave the house again, and cross the road to Endcliffe Park.

These days – outside time – were solitary. I had no companion, no accomplice. Nor did I catch the bus into the city centre to roam among the stores whose offerings I coveted but could rarely afford – Topshop and Chelsea Girl on Fargate, Bradley's Records on Chapel Walk – or the make-up counters at Boots. Instead, I took a book – usually one I wasn't supposed to be reading – and mooched through the park, hoping no one would recognise me or my brown school duffel coat. Sometimes I attempted to smoke one of the cigarettes I'd 'borrowed' from my brother before he'd gone to university in London that autumn. My other brother, the older of the two, had booked a plane ticket to Australia the day after Thatcher had won the election in 1979; he'd been working as a long-distance lorry driver during the previous long winter, known as the Winter of Discontent due to its industrial unrest, and wanted sun and a new start. I hadn't seen him for over a year, although he would write long airmail letters and send photographs of himself, the bush, and his motorbike and dogs. Despite our age gap he was the closest I'd ever had to a soulmate; I missed him terribly.

Endcliffe Park, with its stepping stones, two duck ponds, and dumpy statue of Queen Victoria, usually covered in bird shit (an impolite gesture from nature given that the park was opened in honour of her Jubilee in 1887), gives way to Bingham Park's bowling green and tennis courts, hidden away at the top of a steep grassy bank which, when a small child, I would roll down for the thrill of it. In spring it would be the first place to be covered in daffodils. Heading up the path to Whiteley Woods, past the Shepherd Wheel at Porter Brook, I could be sure to be alone, walking unseen among the trees, watching the people on the path below me. 'To walk invisible' as Charlotte Brontë wrote to her publisher about the advantages of being a pseudonymous author. My limericks had been unsigned, but I had also not intended them to be read. Or had I? I determined to give up writing poetry forever.

There was a big house through the trees, the other side of the stream, the Whiteley Wood Psychiatry Clinic. I knew only a little about psychiatric hospitals in 1980.

At school they were referred to as 'the loony bin', or more generally by the catch-all term 'Middlewood', after Sheffield's largest asylum, opened in 1872 and eventually closed in 1996. Middlewood was enormous, the stuff of nightmares. It was also a building to which my school bore a distinct resemblance. Purpose-built as a girls' school in 1878, it was adorned with turrets and secret rooms and a deconsecrated church which served as a gymnasium – the only modern additions being the science block and the art building. It was situated next door to an ivy-covered private residence with the name 'Thanatos House' inscribed on the gatepost. *Thanatos* – in Greek mythology the personification of death! With this level of material at my disposal, I was primed to be Catherine Morland in Jane Austen's *Northanger Abbey*, 'in training to be a heroine'.

I rarely met anyone on these walks, but once or twice thought I might be being followed. I figured it was my imagination.

It always seemed to be wet and wintry on truant days – perhaps I was happier in summer. If it wasn't raining I'd walk out past Forge Dam and sit on a stile to read my book with the rooks building their witchy nests in the trees high above me, waiting for the café, near what was once a boating lake but was now sinisterly silted up with weeds and algae, to open at ten o'clock. The café was part of a group of former workers' cottages; next to it was a playground with a giant steel slide built into the wall and accessed by vertiginous steps. As a nervous child I had to be coaxed onto it, but my father would always be there at the bottom to catch me.

My truanting ceased once it was deemed imperative that I was collected from school every day. In the run-up to Christmas 1980, women in Leeds were under virtual lockdown. After Jacqueline Hill's murder, a number of female students had left their university courses. The police reaction was to impose a curfew: 'Do not go out at night unless absolutely necessary, and only if accompanied by a man you know.' Women had been fighting back since 1977, when the first UK Reclaim the Night march was organised in Leeds, by the Leeds Revolutionary Feminist Group, partly in response to the Ripper murders. 'No Curfew on Women – Curfew on Men' was the slogan the placards bore.

Years later, as a first-year university student, I was reminded of the curfews when I opened my fresher welcome pack to reveal, alongside the inevitable savoury rice and tub of Pot Noodles, a rape alarm. There was no mention of educating men not to harass women; it was still down to us to protect ourselves, to walk invisible. In Sheffield back in the winter of 1980 my twenty-two-year-old cousin, newly arrived from Australia, had refused to be dictated to, despite my mother's pleas: accustomed to wide-open spaces she would stride out alone after dark.

When my mother woke me in tears on the morning of 9 December, I assumed there had been another murder. There had, but it had taken place in the United States:

John Lennon had been shot dead in New York the night before. The Beatles, and particularly *Sgt. Pepper's Lonely Hearts Club Band*, had been the background music to my early childhood.

Abba's 'Super Trouper' was knocked off the number one spot by Lennon's '(Just Like) Starting Over', from what would be his final album, *Double Fantasy*. By New Year it had been replaced by one of Lennon's previous hits – 'Imagine'. I dug out our family's old singles – 45s with the Apple Corps logo represented by an image of a green Granny Smith apple in the centre. Christmas 1980 resounded to 'Get Back', 'Come Together' and 'Something'. The atmosphere lightened: someone joked that the Ripper had taken a couple of weeks off.

For one of my presents that year, my father had given me a copy of Kate Bush's album *Never Forever*, having first checked, as he said, that there was nothing 'unsuitable' on the printed lyric sheet. The songs on *Never Forever* deal variously with incest, murder, infidelity, ghosts, war, and nuclear annihilation. Perhaps he hadn't been wearing his glasses.

By the time Peter Sutcliffe came to trial the following spring, on 29 April 1981 – my birthday – to be convicted within three weeks and sentenced to life for thirteen murders, there was no question among the press and public that he was the monster of all our nightmares. But as Joan Smith, who had been one of the few women reporters on the case, perceptively wrote later in her essay 'There's Only

One Yorkshire Ripper', 'police in the north of England embarked on a wild goose chase for a man they visualised as a reincarnation of Jack the Ripper. This is the terrible mistake, the appalling blunder, that lies at the heart of the case; this is the real reason why Peter William Sutcliffe was able to roam with impunity through the towns and cities of northern England for more than five years, restlessly searching out his victims: if you devote your resources to tracking down a figure from myth, if you waste your time starting at shadows, you are not likely to come up with a lorry driver from Bradford.'

The testimonies of various of his victims who survived, were ignored; others were maligned by a media obsessed with characterising women – particularly sex workers – as somehow complicit in their own deaths. Sutcliffe himself had been interviewed by the Ripper Squad an astonishing nine times. During one interrogation the same size seven Wellington boot from which a footprint – a crucial piece of evidence – had been found at the scene of the murder of Patricia Atkinson in April 1977, was standing upright in plain sight in Sutcliffe's garage.

Nearly forty years had passed since our family day in Haworth and the Yorkshire Ripper's arrest and trial, when, early on the morning of 13 November 2020, a Sheffield friend texted me simply with the words 'Sutcliffe has died.' By then my father had been dead for over a decade. The person who had been 'Dad' was a memory – a voice on the end of the telephone weeping because he missed tucking me into bed at night. He had also been the cruel father who wouldn't send money for a new winter coat even though my old one was too short and my knees were cold. He became, ever more frequently as the years passed, a remote, almost mythic figure I still longed for – until I didn't.

He left when I was too young to know him as a real person beyond the feelings of abandonment he caused, or to peer behind the myth that I created around him; too many years spent starting at shadows.

Chapter Five

Long Hot Summer

The summer after the spring in which I turned sixteen, I was to be found naked in front of the long mirror in my bedroom. Propped up against the wall, its frame peeling, adorned with faded stickers, the glass gave back to me my ongoing year-long secret project of self-discovery. Ignoring the sounds of traffic outside from nearby Hunter's Bar, I swivelled the frequency on my clock radio to John Peel's show and turned up the volume.

> *The summer she was fifteen, Melanie discovered she was made of flesh and blood. O My America, my new found land. She embarked on a tranced voyage, exploring the whole of herself . . . For hours she stared at herself, naked in the mirror of her wardrobe . . .*

I read Angela Carter greedily, guiltily. Her writing: ornate, baroque and so very wicked. The perfect role model for an emergent self.

Following the example of Melanie in *The Magic Toyshop*, I observed a blue vein in my right breast, or was it the left – the looking-glass reversal was confusing. But then we lived in a looking-glass world, the world of the cold war: everything seemed back to front, unreal, precarious.

The vein was the colour of the Mediterranean Sea in the late afternoon, ultramarine against dead-white skin.

Turn back time a little way. Crete on the last day of 1981, on a school trip (paid for by my eldest brother, who was earning good money in Australia), I darted – in a rather dashing pair of purple corduroy culottes from C&A – among the remains of the palace of Knossos, home to the Labyrinth and the restless Minotaur. The gypsum throne of King Minos still adorned the throne room. I trod wearily, plodding – as befitted its age – along what is allegedly the oldest road in Europe: narrow cobble stones, cypress trees. Cypress wood was used in the building of the palace pillars; and yet the cypress is a symbol of mourning, not of celebration. A place that acts as a reminder for what has been lost and will be lost.

Blue sea, white sand, blue vein, white breast. Turquoise dolphins leaping in frescoes five thousand years old, cup-bearers, fishermen, toreadors, bare-breasted women with elaborate hairstyles. Being at Knossos made me feel as old as time itself. Later, foolishly let loose in the centre of Heraklion for a couple of hours unchaperoned, my classmates and I drank too much retsina in a café, to the backdrop of The Human League's 'Don't You Want Me' – proud that a band from our home city of Sheffield had the Christmas number one, even here, in Greece – were violently sick, and got told off by our harassed teachers.

Blue vein tracking, blue dolphins flickering, frozen in the past against the white wall, rising up and then plummeting to no future.

In Greek mythology, Zeus appeared in the form of a bull to the Phoenician princess Europa, who was busy doing something else at the time – being herself, daydreaming, picking flowers. Attracted by the beautiful white creature, she climbed on its back. And that was that. Abducted, raped, and impregnated. Thanks to Zeus, Europa gave birth to King Minos, and so the Minoan civilisation, and eventually the continent named Europe came into being. *But she was just picking flowers.*

That's one origin story, anyway.

Neither Europe nor any other continent would be around for much longer: conquest isn't civilisation.

My cat, the sole disinterested witness to my disrobing, watched me disdainfully from the bed, gold-green eyes unblinking.

By 1983 the world was in the grip of an ineluctable nuclear threat, with a senile infrastructure in place in the Soviet Union and a seemingly senile president installed in the White House. Over the next year, even Frankie Goes to Hollywood would stop encouraging us to 'Relax' and get firmly on the anti-war front with 'Two Tribes'.

Spring 1980, a year and a half before my visit to Crete, the East German writer Christa Wolf stood on the same spot at the palace of Knossos. Wolf was on a journey, a quest to interrogate the myth of Cassandra, the Trojan priestess of Apollo, doomed to prophesy and not be believed. Her task: to *'ask questions about the historical fate of the Cassandra figure and conditions for the woman writer past and present'*.

Myth and history have a particular way of combining, rather like memoir and real life. What is fiction, and what fact?

Delving into the past to compare the ancient city state of Troy with that of the final paranoid years of the GDR, Wolf was self-admittedly obsessed with Cassandra: *'She, the captive, took me captive . . . Three thousand years – melted away.'* Her obsession sparked my obsession in turn. The result of Wolf's journey was a book based on five lectures entitled 'Conditions of a Narrative' with the fifth lecture turned into a novella, *Cassandra*. Wolf's search ended in Mycenae, to which Cassandra and the other Trojan women were transported by their captors after Troy was defeated and burned. On reaching the citadel there – and according to which version you read – Cassandra and her abductor Agamemnon were murdered by Agamemnon's wife, Clytemnestra, and her lover, Aegisthus. The last things Cassandra saw were the stone lions carved into the gated entrance to the citadel. Cassandra foretold her fate, of course; she *'smelled blood, she felt the full weight of the curse on the House of Atreus'*.

There was a curse on the West, too; we could smell the blood, the loss of all that we knew: a curse of our own making. In late August 1981, a group of some forty women had set off to walk the hundred or so miles from

Cardiff City Hall to the recently announced site of the US Cruise missile base at Greenham Common near Newbury in Berkshire. Arriving at the base in the early morning of 5 September, they read out their demands to the bewildered policeman at the entrance who had assumed them to be the cleaners arriving early for their shift.

Then four of the women chained themselves to the nine-mile perimeter fence.

An omnipresent fear of nuclear conflict dominated much of the political, cultural and popular thinking of the 1980s. Any self-respecting left-thinking teenager scared witless by the government's feeble 'Protect and Survive' pronouncements and the menace of the Four Minute Warning alarm – the inference being that if you grab a can of baked beans and hide under a table then you too could outlive a nuclear winter – took some solace in the belief that disarmament was the way forward, and vigorous protest the likeliest method of achieving that. The superpowers were set on a collision course equipped with weapons, but the people, and women in particular, were protesting with their bodies.

Writing a journal entry several months after her visit to Greece, in February 1981, Wolf noted: '*Now you no longer need to be "Cassandra" now people can see what is coming.*'

The women of Greenham Common were Cassandra, they could see what was coming. Despised and dismissed by the media, politicians and large sections of the public, and inspiring thousands of others, the growing camp at Greenham would, almost by accident, become a key political battlefield of the cold war's last refuge: the nuclear face-off.

At sixteen, I saw myself slipping easily into the Cassandra role. No one ever listened to me, either.

In tribute to Cassandra and the women of Greenham I composed a song (working title: 'Cassandra and the Women of Greenham') in the style of Kate Bush and played it mercilessly on the piano.

In the next room, my mother sighed and turned the TV up louder.

I needed to do more than attempt to write songs.

As a small child I used to tickle statues in museums; now, held in the mirror's gaze, I stood completely still for as long as possible to practise being one. George Bernard Shaw's *Pygmalion* was the set text for English Literature O-level: the origin of the play's title was more interesting to me than Shaw's examination of class and social mobility. Pygmalion, the misogynist sculptor who created Galatea, an ideal woman, out of ivory.

Angela Carter, among other writers I was reading, subverted this notion of idealism, much as Shaw does in his version of the story. These writers were the antidote to much of what I was taught at that time, or what was shown to me.

Christa Wolf wrote, somewhat disapprovingly: '*It is worth thinking about, why women today feel they must derive part of their self-esteem and a justification of their claims from the fact that civilisation begins with the worship of women.'*

I pulled on some clothes, hastily; someone was knocking at the door of my bedroom.

Having concentrated on particular parts of my body for so long (everything from the chest down: face was too spotty to love, nose humongous), my narcissism had missed what should have been my own prophecy, a strange, almost imperceptible swelling at the front of my neck, like a swan's. By the end of the year such was the transformation effected that I avoided looking at myself naked again: it would be years before I could summon up more than a hurried, disappointed glance.

It was the beginning of a long, hot summer. On the outskirts of Fulwood, lapwings and skylarks swooped over the drowsy Mayfield Valley. On Clarkehouse Road, at the main entrance to the botanical gardens near school, the ice-cream van was always busy. After exams each afternoon, my friend Nora and I queued up for sophisticated mint Cornettos (99s had been relegated to childhood, along with orange ice lollies) and wandered the paths and lawns, shabby and neglected like all our favourite places. I no longer climbed the statue of the god Pan in the rose garden to furtively kiss his cold metal lips as I did as a child, or ran from the imagined terrors of the Victorian bear pit, its dark recesses containing the ghost of a poor lumbering bear, rattling in its chains for over a century.

The gardens opened in 1836, built to a design won in competition by Robert Marnock, gardener at Bretton Hall in Wakefield. The beautiful glasshouses, known as the Paxton Pavilions, were named after Joseph Paxton, then working at Chatsworth House in Derbyshire and later designer of The Crystal Palace, built in Hyde Park to house the Great Exhibition of 1851. The palace was afterwards moved to Sydenham, south London. As a child in Slough, my father witnessed the palace burn down through the night of 30 November 1936: the flames could be seen across eight counties.

The glasshouses in Sheffield were near-derelict, with random broken panes, as if someone had been aimlessly throwing stones. The aviary's two miserable African parrots, each with one leg in an iron ring, were clamped mournfully to their perches, blue, grey, and red plumage bedraggled and dusty. No one knew how old they were. The aviary and the aquarium were created in two of the glasshouses in the early 1950s as a result of War Damage money – reparations for Sheffield's suffering during the Blitz. In the stuffy aquarium, dark sinister shapes moved behind dirty glass, the only light coming from the blue, red, and silver flashes of the tiny neon tetras.

Further down the gardens, the bronze metal statue of Victory stood high on its plinth. Victory commemorated the fallen of Sheffield in the Crimean War of 1854–6. Twenty-two thousand British soldiers died in the war, mostly of disease. Sheffield supplied armaments as well as troops to the Crimean war effort. Henry Bessemer, a prolific inventor (his Bessemer converter changed the face of steel production forever), used his steelworks in the city to create a new type of artillery shell, in the shape of a rocket.

More means of destruction, more ingenious ways in which to injure and kill.

After Russia was defeated at the siege of Sebastopol, and up until war officially ended in April 1856, Sheffield celebrated with gas illuminations, processions, banners, a public holiday, and somewhat tasteless hangings of effigies of the Emperor of Russia. Grinders produced knives engraved with the names of battle victories, workhouse inmates were allowed 'unlimited' roast beef. The *pièce de résistance* of all this fanfare was a Crimean 'monstre cake' weighing four tons, created by confectioner George Bassett, and commissioned by a local entrepreneur. Due to its size, the cake was carried through the city balanced on three wagons travelling abreast. The icing alone weighed 412 pounds. Complaints about the quality of the cake, which was not properly cooked, came thick and fast. 'A proportion of the cake was really excellent, but a large quantity of it was unfit to eat,' griped one letter to the *Sheffield Daily Telegraph*.

Perhaps the moral here is that gorging on dubious victory inevitably leaves a bad taste.

The need for nationalistic and patriotic celebration is peculiar to war, a collective public show of mania to hide the human cost. Entries for the South Yorkshire Lunatic Asylum, opened in 1872, bleakly gave the following cause of insanity for a number of patients: '*Sons having gone to the Crimean War.*'

One son was George Partington, whose headstone in the General Cemetery included his Crimean helmet, carved in stone. (George Bassett, of the 'monstre cake' and Bassett's Liquorice Allsorts fame, is also buried there.) George Partington survived the Battle of Balaclava and also action at Inkerman and Sebastopol. After Balaclava he was cared for by Florence Nightingale. I would frequently pass George's grave and extravagant stone helmet on my trips to the cemetery, sitting on the broken chapel steps – the chapel was my own citadel, my personal House of Atreus. There I would smoke and read T.S. Eliot's *Four Quartets* out loud to the straggling weeds, the crows, the tombs, the urns, and the silent interred. Often Nora and I would meet there, and we'd choke on our attempts to inhale Sobranie Black Russian cigarettes with gold tips, swigging whisky that burned our throats from a bottle one of us had purloined.

By the summer of 1983, the chapel had been boarded up, eliminating all evidence of the afternoon the summer before when I had drunkenly daubed 'HELLO DARKNESS' on the back wall, using a discarded can of paint found nearby. Perhaps it would be excavated one day, like Pompeii or the frescoes at Knossos, revealing my crappy vandalism from thousands of years before. Except the planet wouldn't last another thousand years. Or a hundred years. Or even ten.

❀

Nora and I lay side by side on the hot grass of the botanical gardens, listening to the bees in the lavender and slowly relishing our Cornettos. *To live alone, in the bee-loud glade.*

We didn't really have much in common. Almost everyone at school, with very few exceptions, supported 'Mrs Thatcher' and believed emphatically in the nuclear 'deterrent'. Greenham and the camp there were dismissed as irrelevant. In the eyes of my classmates and their parents I came from a hotbed of left-wing activists, evidenced by the fact that my mother was a member of the local Labour party. Worse, she had friends who in the recent general election in June had campaigned to be elected to two notoriously Tory Derbyshire seats. Neither succeeded: the Conservatives capitalised on the jingoistic spirit unleashed by the Falklands War of the previous year to romp home with a landslide victory.

Yet Nora and I shared a hatred of school and a private intensity. We wrote each other letters on stiff multicoloured paper bought from the Athena shop in York, in gold and silver ink, which alluded to – in rather formal but passionate prose – the things we didn't care to discuss in person. My mother, who plucked these missives from the front doormat twice a week, asked me why I was writing to myself, which I crossly denied. Looking more closely, I realised what she meant: Nora's handwriting was the mirror image of mine, with its Greek epsilons and alphas. A distortion.

I had received another letter earlier in the summer, from a different source. After several torturous years of access visits, and shortly after my sixteenth birthday, an age when I finally acquired some quasi-legal control over my decisions in this matter, I had got up the courage, if it can be called that – in fact cowardice might be a better word – to write to my father, because I couldn't put what I needed to say in direct speech. What I was unable to express, even in writing, was that our fortnightly meetings, a form of verbal arm-to-arm combat with me very much on the losing side, made me ill with anxiety, to the point that I no longer saw a point to carrying on with them, at least not for now. Instead, I wrote that with revising and exams coming up, I was too busy to see him; as if I had ever worked hard for anything, never mind exams. Perhaps I should have anticipated my father's response. Much of his letter I blocked out immediately, for reasons of self-preservation. At the time I couldn't see his pain, I only felt his anger: set down in black ink, by a pen pressed vehemently into the paper. I knew then as I know now that it was not the sort of letter a parent should write to their child, but we had not been on familiar or safe ground for some years now.

I took the letter to the General Cemetery and proceeded to burn it ceremonially on the steps outside the chapel, using the same match to light my Sobranie. I didn't particularly enjoy smoking, but that wasn't what it was about. It was about style and finesse, something ineffable, to be enjoyed like the TV adaptation of *Brideshead Revisited*, the luxurious drama of which swept me along while scoffing at the toffs. The small fire crackled and the black ink danced in the flames, my father's extravagant handwriting, with its emphatic loops, disappearing into ashes. My throat hurt, furry, like the bodies of the drugged moths and butterflies which my friend Gabrielle, a self-styled lepidopterist, pinned to her silly board; thick with tears that wouldn't come. Walled off, boarded up, like the chapel behind me, I sat on alone.

My mother said nothing further about the letters from Nora, but, as was usual when she wanted to make a point or show understanding, she left a book in my room which 'you might like to read'. Before my periods began this was a slim volume titled *Have You Started Yet?* to which I had responded with a note back on which I wrote 'No, I Haven't.' This time, it was a novel by Deborah Hautzig with the bizarre title *Hey, Dollface!* I picked it up, despite myself. The book, set in late 1970s New York City, focuses on the friendship between two fifteen-year-olds, Val and Chloe. The pair share a dislike of their snooty Manhattan private school and hang out in local cemeteries and thrift stores. Chloe and Val were essentially and uncannily the American version of Nora and me.

We, or rather I, had been frequenting our own thrift store, The Front Parlour on Sharrow Vale Road, for a while. The Front Parlour was a tiny emporium selling everything from the past: linen, Art Deco vases, trinkets, clocks, lamps, cigarette cases, hip flasks, hat pins, glassware, clothes, hats, gloves, lingerie, jewellery. The clothes – whether a rare, beaded flapper dress, or a beaver lamb fur coat – could be tried on discreetly behind a tiny screen. I saved up for a 1920s black astrakhan hat which I wore with a peacock feather tucked into the brim, the drawing of which I alone considered to be the star of my O-level art submission. Betty Nash, the shop's owner, was always exquisitely dressed in a 1940s nipped-in black suit, pearl earrings and red lipstick. Known as 'the Coco Chanel of Sharrow Vale Road', Mrs Nash and her shop influenced my approach to clothes and style just as much as 1980s style bibles such as *The Face* or *i-D* magazine, or my sister's copies of *Vogue*.

Retired were my dungarees, Dexys records and the polka-dot ra-ra skirt that I had worn with black footless tights the year before when we were all obsessed with *Fame*. Now I had a turquoise pinstriped dress with leg-of-mutton buttoned sleeves and a long, dark red wraparound skirt from the Laura Ashley sale. Colours released me: the past couple of winters had been monochrome outside and in. With cold, stiff hands I would linger in the kitchen, attempting to dye my clothes black with Dylon, either in the washing machine – which no one else could then use – or leaving them to soak murkily in buckets by the back door. My attention then turned to my hair. After some attempts with Crazy Color to 'discreetly' turn the ends purple, the campaign of self-transformation moved on to the bathroom towels, which were soon covered in henna stains. A glorious gloop of henna solidified on my head every few months, bilious-green and foul smelling,

wafting through the landing on the first floor as I saun-
tered back to my bedroom and my cassette player on
which Ultravox enthused me to 'Reap the Wild Wind'.

As *Hey, Dollface!* continues, the girls' relationship devel-
ops. Val and Chloe are curious, confused, and intimate,
although any deeper physicality is lightly brushed over
– the book is less about a tentative exploration of sexuality
and more about the kind of ardent friendship common to
teenagers. It all comes to a head when Chloe's suspicious
mother walks in and misconstrues a scene. Mostly, after
reading it, I wanted desperately to visit the thrift stores of
New York. But I was mortified, too. Did my mother think
I was gay? Had she seen me reading Colette's *Claudine*
novels too avidly? And what did I feel for Nora, anyway?
It was less physical than emotional. On occasions we'd
been tipsy and held hands, I'd experienced a shiver of
excitement but not thought of anything more. My desire
was general, vague, inchoate, and reacted to proximity.
At school gender conformity and heterosexuality were
presumed if not tacitly enforced. For all my prolific
reading – which by now included Anaïs Nin's *Delta of
Venus* and Erica Jong's *Fear of Flying*, smuggled from the
bookshelves in our living room – I was extremely naive.
'What's a zipless fuck?' I had once asked, innocently,
during a family dinner.

We had a new lodger in his late twenties and I knew
I was attracted to him – but again it was primarily
emotional. I shared none of this with my mother; we
didn't talk about the book, but there were quite a few

arrangements made to keep me busy that summer, both at home and away from Sheffield.

There was also a fact of which Nora and I were very aware: I would be going to a different school for sixth form, armed with what paltry clutch of O-levels I could muster – minus maths. After gaining a mere 6 per cent in the mock, 'the worst result in the history of the school', I had been banned from taking the actual exam. At the time I boasted of this achievement.

For my birthday at the end of April, just before the start of the exams, I received a pair of long, cerise-coloured vintage satin evening gloves with a rich, sticky lipstick to match, and my first grown-up perfume, Guerlain's Mitsouko. Patting it on to my all-important 'pulse points', I cut my hair in an uneven fringe across my forehead, after studying photographs of my namesake, a frankly emaciated Katherine Mansfield, in her kimono.

At this pre-official adult age, my apparent 'freedoms' included the opportunity to leave school, get married (with my parents' permission, so no point in that, who wants their parents' permission for anything?), change my name by deed poll, and have sex.

Allegedly, the possibilities were endless. Or they would have been if we weren't all going to die in a nuclear inferno.

Things were hotting up at Greenham. On 1 April, some 70,000 people had linked arms to create a human chain between three nuclear arms bases in Berkshire: Greenham Common, the atomic weapons factory at Burghfield, and the atomic weapons research establishment at Aldermaston, scene of the anti-nuclear marches of the 1950s and 1960s. The peaceful protest, in which demonstrators handed out Easter daffodils to police officers, and prams and pushchairs, carrying the babies and small children of those protesting, were festooned with balloons, was condemned by the defence secretary, Michael Heseltine, as 'naive and reckless'. Heseltine suggested that by demanding unilateral disarmament protesters were playing directly into the hands of the Kremlin. Both sides claimed victory. The April protest sparked others across Europe. Greenham was now international news.

I wouldn't be going on to sixth form in the new school after the summer, I informed my mother, blithely. There was no point.

She didn't bat an eyelid, just said fine, and how would I earn my living?

I had no answer to this.

So it was decided. I would be leaving *this* school and going to *that* school. It was sort of my choice, although not really. There was no more money to be borrowed to cover the fees. Exams were nearing an end. Defying school rules, I had sat each one plastered in eye make-up from the Mary Quant palette my sister bought me for luck – a gold and brown ensemble which made me look like an alarming bee. Clashing earrings of pink and blue titanium, also forbidden, swung from my ears. On my way to one exam I passed the headmistress in the corridor and instead of admonishing me as usual she looked straight through me: I no longer existed for her; I was leaving, I had not brought honours to the school, I was not wealthy. Ultimately, I was a nuisance. 'You'll never get a job being good at English' she had once told me, with an undertone of triumph.

Decades have passed, but I continue to dream about that place, where I was incarcerated for nine conflicted years. The high, forbidding church-like windows of the main hall through which the sun glared scathingly at us prisoners; the annexe from the main Victorian building to the modern science block; the end of the path near the gymnasium, where we smoked illicit cigarettes, and where, when bold (I was never bold), meetings with boys from the comprehensive across the road occurred; the internecine warfare that masqueraded as hockey practice on the school playing field. The walls surrounding the playing field were embedded at the top with broken glass – to keep intruders out, or ourselves in; I was never certain which.

One place I did not venture to was Melbourne Avenue, the lane snaking alongside the back of the playing field. How could it still be there? Ever since the Ripper was caught that cold January night in 1981 it had been tainted.

Point the way into the darkness. Into the slaughterhouse. And alone.

Cassandra again, flickering and dying out.

Back in the botanical gardens that mid-June afternoon, I rifled through the dirty hessian bag which once belonged to a brother and had recently replaced my school satchel. The bag was scrawled all over with quotations daubed in ink and embellished with badges shouting slogans such as 'Nuclear Power? No Thanks' or the enigmatic (I was constantly aiming for enigmatic) statement 'Everything Contains Its Opposite'.

Lying on the grass, gazing up at the fathomless blue sky over this small safe space within our big vulnerable city, my thoughts were on war. I recalled the fairy tale I was most disturbed by as a child: the story of Chicken Licken, who – along with various other animals he meets along the way – is on a mission to tell the king that the sky is falling.

I shivered under the hot sun. My Cornetto was finished. Without taking my eyes off the sky, I said to Nora: 'I'm going to Greenham Common.' She propped herself up on one elbow and stared at me. 'What?'

That summer of 1983, the protests at Greenham, although loud, were non-violent. Women came from all over to support the growing camp, first in their hundreds and then in their thousands. Since the initial descent on the Common in early autumn 1981, debates were held following the Quaker tradition of speaking by turn. It took two years of 'dialogue and philosophising' before the decision was taken to break in by cutting the perimeter fence which surrounded the base with bolt cutters. These were referred to under the code name 'black cardigans'. Once inside the base, it would only be a short time before each protester was removed and arrested for criminal damage. For many, it was their first experience of direct action. The majority of the women had never been in trouble with the courts before. Yet here they were, becoming expert in conducting their own defences, invoking myriad bylaws and ancient common- ers' rights, arguing with the local magistrates and even with the US presidency that the very existence of the missiles amounted to a genocidal act. Refusing to pay fines, they instead elected to go to prison; once released, their protest resumed.

Incidentally, one of the Newbury magistrates who reg- ularly handed out fines to the protestors was the mother of a future Conservative prime minister, David Cameron.

Families were left, degree courses and jobs put on hold – sometimes for years – as a result of this commit- ment, a commitment that was dismissed by detractors as a foolhardy enterprise but which many of the partici- pants considered the most empowering experience of their lives. The publicity generated was incredible. The women's bright clothes were a deliberate life-affirming contrast to the dull camouflage of the base's soldiers, echoed by the banners – some basic, some beautifully embroidered – which emerged from many local CND and women's groups across the UK. Soon various distinct camps were set up at each gate, named for the colours of the rainbow. The 'Yellow' gate attracted the great- est notoriety and housed the hard-line protesters; the

'Turquoise' gate was strictly vegan, whereas meat-eaters congregated at the 'Violet' gate. The first mass demonstration at Greenham – 'Embrace the Base' – took place on 12 December 1982. Thirty-five thousand women encircled the perimeter fence, holding hands, singing and attaching flowers, pictures, scarves and even tampons to 'our Berlin wall'.

Meanwhile I was plotting, I was planning; at least in theory. More than anything else, because it was my default activity, I was reading. Women were centre-stage in this battle, and the books I chose echoed this. Our generation had been primed for some vague impending disaster all our lives; most of us were born during the Vietnam War. The capture of Saigon from the US military by the People's Army of Vietnam and the Viet Cong, in late April 1975, and subsequent evacuation and airlifts of refugees, had been one of my first media memories.

In the UK that same year Peter Dickinson's children's science-fiction trilogy *The Changes* was adapted and shown on television. In *The Changes* an all-encompassing, increasingly unbearable high-pitched noise, causing a form of mass tinnitus, begins to emanate from any kind of mechanised device – cars, buses, trains, televisions, radios, factories, tractors, electricity pylons – leading most of the population to abandon and violently destroy technology and attempt to live in a pre-industrial age. *The Changes* was anarchic and nightmare-inducing television, because it seemed so plausible, and its weird, volatile energy was infectious, leaping off the screen.

Parallel to this I was reading a new book set much closer to home. Sheffield author Linda Hoy's novel *The Damned* was written in the white heat of the differing strategies of the anti-nuclear movement. Seventeen-year-old Chris is a member of the group D.A.M.N., which advocates violent tactics to thwart the nuclear programme. When he meets Sarah, a feminist and pacifist, he is forced to examine his involvement with D.A.M.N. Sarah's poise and self-control, even if smug and self-righteous, and her refusal to be cowed by an increasingly scary male agenda, seemed heroic.

I was reading and thinking, for certain, but as the summer progressed I was still nowhere nearer to Greenham despite my declared intention to Nora.

In early July I travelled to London. Months before, my mother had bought tickets (by cutting out and sending off a coupon from *The Observer*) for my brother and me to see David Bowie in concert as part of his 'Serious Moonlight' tour to promote the *Let's Dance* album.

On the train, I found a table seat and tried to relax – I wasn't used to travelling this far alone. Deep into my book, and a voice opposite demanded to know what I was reading. A large, perspiring man had chosen to sit directly across from me, despite the rest of the carriage being almost completely empty. The book, recently published by Virago Press, had its self-explanatory title clearly marked on the cover: *Over Our Dead Bodies: Women Against the Bomb*. I pointed to it and carried on reading.

The man persisted. What was my name, my age, was I travelling by myself, did I have a boyfriend. I answered monosyllabically and untruthfully, willing him to go away.

When the ticket inspector emerged, I gazed up at him in silent pleading, hoping he would help me out of my predicament. Nothing. The stranger snatched up my Young Person's Railcard, and he and the ticket inspector agreed it was a nice photograph, but that I was prettier *in the flesh*. They laughed. I tried to make myself as small as possible in my seat. As the inspector moved away down the carriage, my unsolicited travelling companion smiled broadly at me. With his eyes dreamily and firmly fixed on my miserable face, his hand moved rapidly down his body to where, hidden by the table between us, it began to make vigorous jerking movements. I jumped up, grabbed my bag, and ran in the opposite direction through several carriages, locking myself in the nearest toilet for the rest of the journey, In that stuffy, sour-smelling space I continued reading my book with a blank ferocity.

But she was just picking flowers.

The essays in *Over Our Dead Bodies* are from women of all ages, classes, circumstances, backgrounds. They include Dorothy Thompson, the historian of working-class history, and wife of the socialist and peace campaigner E.P. Thompson; Angela Carter – on Goya's 'black' paintings; Marjorie Mowlam, then a politics lecturer at Newcastle University and the future Secretary of State for Northern Ireland; students, activists, novelists and philosophers.

Most memorably and urgently, Carter wrote, paraphrasing Dylan Thomas: 'War is no longer the province of men and as its most vulnerable potential victims we must arm ourselves – not with weapons but with rage, rage as if against the dying of the light.'

At St Pancras, my brother, who had just finished his university finals, wove his way, perched on an old bicycle, onto the platform to meet me. Relieved to see him, I didn't mention what had happened on the train, distracted by the soot-grimed Gothic glory of St Pancras station, dilapidated and near-derelict after decades of neglect, home to strutting pigeons, its corners full of people with nowhere else to go, its platforms solely for trains to and from Sheffield and Nottingham. A station which only served the East Midlands, a London space full of Northern accents. From an open window nearby the sound of Billy Idol's 'Hot in the City' drifted down to the streets below, cluttered with people and rubbish.

The heat in London was stifling. Dirty air. The next morning, we made our way by train to Milton Keynes where we walked, or rather processed, to the concert venue – the Milton Keynes Bowl. I had a nagging blister on my heel due to a pair of too-small fake leopard-skin stiletto heels, a recent purchase from The Front Parlour. We sat on the top of a balding, once grassy bank with thousands of others under the beating midday sun, peering down at the stage far below and the tiny figure of David Bowie, his shock of white-blond hair. My brother knew every song – even 'Red Sails', from the *Lodger* album – and wrote them all down in biro on a scrap of paper for me. Bowie was deeply, knowingly theatrical. For his performance of 'Cracked Actor', he held a skull in his hand – I so hoped it was an actual human skull – and addressed it with a line from Hamlet: 'Alas, poor Yorick!' before launching into the song.

On the train home to Sheffield, with Bowie's 'Fantastic Voyage' and Grace Jones's 'Slave to the Rhythm' – which had been pounding from my brother's record player – competing for room in my head, I picked a busy carriage. No one had better come near me.

Later in July, my sixteenth birthday treat: two weeks in Paris with my mother. As usual money was tight, so we travelled the cheapest and hottest way possible – the coach from Sheffield's Pond Street bus station to London, then another coach to Dover, hovercraft to Calais and a final coach on to Paris. When we eventually arrived in central Paris, the leaves of its famous plane trees deflated in the still humid early evening, we were met by Camille. Almost a part of our family: I could not recall a time when I didn't know Camille. Her older sister had been my sister's penfriend, and Camille in turn became the penfriend of my eldest brother. When she first stayed with us in Sheffield in the early 1970s, aged about fourteen, my father had politely inquired what she would like to drink. 'Whisky' was not the response he had anticipated.

Bedraggled and sticky next to her cool sophistication, we travelled with her by Métro west across the city to where she lived alone in a small block of flats in the suburb of Courbevoie, next to La Défense, the business district. From La Défense's main plaza we could see all the way down the extended Axe historique to the glittering diamond-like strand of the Champs Elysées with the Arc de Triomphe resplendently visible at the end. As guests, we slept in the living/dining room, each with a narrow bed at either end – my mother's was the sofa, mine a sort of cot – assembled every evening and restored to daytime furniture in the morning. My bed was directly next to the window: awake most nights with an inexplicably pounding heart, I looked out on polluted skies, extravagant sunrises and mighty thunderstorms. Lying rigid, swaddled in the sheet, arms by my sides, I would await the ritual descent of the tiny black creatures amassed on the ceiling above me. Every morning I would find several new bites to scratch and gouge, on my arms, neck, legs – any chink in my shroud was a target.

The days passed in a haze. My mother was preoccupied, I was strangely tired, and truculent: often we just didn't get on. We were out all day in Paris, with a packed lunch of sliced baguette, a hunk of squishy Brie, tomatoes and a flask of black coffee: sometimes with Camille, usually just the two of us. My mother and I walked for hours in the atrophying heat. I was relieved that I had insisted – not without some argument – on bringing my large green-and-yellow-striped umbrella all the way from Sheffield; it made for a perfect sunshade.

We traded outings: we would traipse all the way to the 20th arrondissement and Père Lachaise cemetery so that

I could pay homage at Jim Morrison's grave if we could also queue for entry for the last days of the big Manet retrospective at Le Petit Palais, held to mark the centenary of his death.

The Manet was the first major art show I had seen and it moved me far more than the tombs of Père Lachaise – unthinkable though it seemed, I was possibly growing out of hanging around graveyards, although that summer I experienced an abundance of them. I was especially excited to see the real *Le Déjeuner sur l'herbe* after Bow Wow Wow's controversial-doesn't-cover-it photographic 'remake' to accompany their 1982 single 'Go Wild in the Country'. The controversy stemmed from the fact that the band's singer and naked poser was only fifteen. Annabella Lwin had been 'discovered' singing along to a radio in a launderette by pop impresario Malcolm McLaren, who had managed the Sex Pistols and Adam and the Ants. At school the majority view was that Bow Wow Wow were ridiculous, although there was a sneaking appreciation of Annabella's directly voiced desire on the trash-pop single 'I Want Candy'. After all, she was our age: we all felt that way about men in sweaters.

We fitted as much as possible into the days: a trip to Auvers-sur-Oise, where we saw the graves of Van Gogh and his brother Theo, two white headstones very close to each other, covered with a thick carpet of ivy like a giant eiderdown, as if the brothers had just been tucked in for the night; a cinema trip to see vampire film of the moment *The Hunger*; a night at the Left Bank's famous

English-language bookshop Shakespeare & Co, where we met its owner/proprietor George Whitman; a dinner in Belleville with French-Algerian friends of Camille's, one of whom treated us to an impromptu performance of belly dancing.

Paris still sizzled, but our visit was almost over. It was the second week of August; my exam results were imminent. My mother and I made one final expedition – to Fontainebleau, not for its grand chateau, but for the New Zealand writer Katherine Mansfield, my name-sake, who died of tuberculosis on 9 January 1923, aged thirty-four, while staying nearby at Gurdjieff's Institute for Harmonious Development of Man. My mother was dismissive of Gurdjieff, an Armenian philosopher and spiritual leader. Like many, she viewed him as a dangerous crank, his emphasis on spartan living conditions and hard labour highly unsuitable for a terminally ill patient such as Mansfield. Mansfield herself was positive about her weeks at the Institute, where she seemed to spend much of her time in freezing and insanitary conditions peeling countless carrots for the meagre communal meal, hovering around a pigsty and, for several hours each day, lying suspended above a cow manger (an unproven remedy advised by the spiritual adviser). When her husband John Middleton Murry visited her, on the day she died, he described Mansfield as 'radiant' – although that could have been because she was weakened through lack of nourishment and heat, and inappropriate physical work. '*It is intensely cold here*' is the only near-complaint that breaks into her last letters, like a sob. In the end sentences have become too much; her scribblings are fragmented: *'I am cold, bring paper to light a fire . . . wood . . . flame . . . strength . . . light a fire . . . no more fire. Because there is no more fire.'*

It was almost five o'clock by the time we reached the small cemetery at Avon where Mansfield was buried. The concierge with his set of iron keys was about to close up for the day, but relented when my mother told him we had come all the way from New Zealand (which, in one sense we had) to see Mansfield's grave. The man pointed us in the general direction and we stopped when his shouts of *'là-bas, là-bas'* ceased. My mother took a photo of me by the grave, which, when developed, seemed almost of Mansfield's era – frizzy piled-up hair, long red skirt fastened at the waist with an old leather belt and brass buckle, ivory blouse with broderie-anglaise sleeves, which for reasons of 'style', I was wearing back to front. We noted the inscription on the headstone, a favourite quotation of Katherine's from Shakespeare's *Henry IV Part I*: 'But I tell you, my lord fool, out of this nettle, danger, we pluck this flower, safety.' A life lived in risk, cut off too soon. As we walked out of the cemetery I touched my throat, my fingers brushing over the small but steadily growing lump which had, by now, been there for some time.

The next morning, feet stained red with the dye from the cheap shoes I had been tramping about in, I could not get out of bed. I had never felt so tired in my life: as if I had been drugged. My body was no longer the body of the previous day, but another, parallel body, its unaccountable heaviness weighing me down.

My mother was concerned – we had overdone it – the heat, and an excess of morbid trips to graveyards. I lay on my cot and read Alain-Fournier's *Le Grand Meaulnes*, the author's single novel, published in 1913 – he was killed aged twenty-seven in the first month of the carnage of the First World War – about a once-visited, now lost chateau, an impressionable young hero, a beautiful unattainable woman. It's to be read now, and then again when you're old, my mother had told me, but after closing the book and its heady prose – a last gasp of Romanticism before the world changed forever – I didn't think I would return to it. Not even if I reached old age.

Sheffield was also locked in heat, but without the beautiful architecture or the Seine. Ignoring the pile of multi-coloured envelopes awaiting me from Nora, with whom I had hardly communicated over the last three weeks and felt a growing distance from, I retreated to the spare attic room. Most of the rest of August was spent humming along to the Style Council's *Long Hot Summer* EP. Paul Weller's jazzy rendition of 'Paris Match' took me back to the recent holiday and, still impossibly tired, I dozed the afternoons away on the attic bed, fondling my swelling neck. I had swapped Sobranies for unfiltered Gauloises, and spat out the strings of tobacco as I sipped my instant Nescafé coffee, made strong with four teaspoons. No wonder my heart beat so fast these late August days, almost in rhythm to the music. I brooded over Françoise Sagan's cold, calculating *Bonjour Tristesse* and passed through the ritual fire that is Sylvia Plath's *The Bell Jar.*

I was in abeyance.

My O-level results arrived in the post – unsatisfactory, but they would do. I could take my preferred subjects for A-level. The weather broke: the situation, in stagnation all summer, started to shift.

At the very end of the month I met Nora (the date and time set, appropriately, by letter) in the drenched botanical gardens, by the Pan statue. The friendship which had seemed so necessary a year ago was now curdled and claustrophobic; I wanted to kill it, with my transfer to a new school as the excuse. I was using my striped umbrella for its proper purpose but had not replaced my cheap, non-waterproof red shoes. In the pouring rain the colour drained swiftly from them like blood from a frightened face. I do not remember what was said between Nora and me, huddled in our raincoats, or if we even looked at each other. As I walked away towards the turnstile exit of the gardens, behind the bear pit, releasing me to Brocco Bank and home, I do remember that the sun came out and a half-rainbow emerged. I started to whistle. I did not see Nora again. She telephoned for weeks afterwards, but I wouldn't speak to her. Somehow, I had learned to be cruel, and I didn't feel particularly good about it.

Given the clumsiness with which I'd ended my friendship with Nora, I fully deserved for sixth form to go badly, yet after the initial shock of its size and numbers, the opposite happened. The first morning I had stood conspicuously alone in the sixth-form common room upon arrival. No one spoke to me, and I lasted about ten petrified minutes before turning round and catching the bus back home. But on the second day the sympathetic deputy head assigned Natalie and Fay to me, an action which began a friendship that would last decades. I had a social life, I was talking to boys without blushing, I was making friends, ones who didn't consider being left wing 'unpatriotic'. We had a tuck shop in the common room – basically a hatch – and bought toast and instant coffee, Curly Wurlys and Wagon Wheels for three pence. At Christmas the dinner ladies handed out mince pies and satsumas. At lunchtimes we often went round the corner from school to Natalie's, buying chip butties to eat on the way. Fridays were the big night and I queued up with everyone else at the B-hive on West Street and requested the same order: a half of cider and black. Not wearing a uniform, having Wednesday afternoons free instead of being forced onto a hockey or netball pitch, having a locker with my own key: the sense of impending adulthood was euphoric.

I was eating more. In fact, I was eating more than I ever had, compulsively. My favourite snack was banana and honey on toast, usually indulged in after everyone else had gone to bed. I roamed the house searching for food like a small hungry bear, trying to quiet my irregular heartbeat. Having always been slight, and even underweight – as a child I would pick at my food – this increase was noticeable. As was the breathlessness.

The contrast with our new lodger, Niamh, was striking. A mature student at the university, Niamh appeared to subsist on a daily diet of Weetabix, tuna, pasta, sweetcorn and cigarettes. I spent many hours in the front attic, now Niamh's room – where I had so recently passed the late summer dreaming and drowsing – attempting to glean vital information about the condition of being a liberated twenty-something woman in the early 1980s. Niamh was part of a women's group and had already been to Greenham several times. I had allowed my interest in the camp to lapse somewhat, but now it sparked up again. *Here was a way in.*

Over that year of 1983 the filmmaker Beeban Kidron had been living among the women of the camp, filming their daily lives and their tense interactions with the police guarding the precious perimeter fence. The result, *Carry Greenham Home* (also a song by the folk singer and Greenham supporter Peggy Seeger), was distributed by Kidron and her co-director Amanda Richardson. It was shown not in mainstream cinemas but in church halls, classrooms, at local peace and women's groups. I attended a screening with Niamh. There was a jubilation to the women on film, an irresistible bravery, similar to that of the Reclaim the Night marches during the Ripper years. Now, the police stood sentinel, darkly anonymous outlines, their attitude patronising, scornful, quickly turning to violence. The women carried on laughing and singing as their tents were kicked in and their companions dragged away.

Doing the cinema rounds at the same time was Richard Eyre's film *The Ploughman's Lunch*. With a screenplay by a rising literary star called Ian McEwan, the film, about the Thatcherite rise of an amoral British journalist, played by Jonathan Pryce, was set in 1982, with the media dominated by coverage of the Falklands War. In one scene, returning from a weekend in Norfolk, Pryce's character's car succumbs to a tyre puncture. Forced to seek help at a nearby peace camp, the journalist agrees to mention the camp's aims back in the office as part of the daily news meeting. When it comes to it, he dismisses the camp as immaterial. The news cycle moves on, without interest. That snippet from *The Ploughman's Lunch* typified so much of the attitude towards the Greenham women as trivial time-wasters, dole-scroungers, unfit mothers and so on – a natural extension of the Conservative government's war on anyone who didn't conform to their necessary ideal of a nuclear family, with heavy irony on the word 'nuclear'.

The tabloid and right-wing press delighted in portraying the Greenham incumbents as dirty, man-hating, aggressive lesbians. The women *were* often dirty – it is impossible to keep clean when your home is a makeshift tent liable to be sliced up by a bailiff at any moment, and you have no ready supply of hot water – and many were lesbian. Some did hold separatist beliefs – though it was later felt that differences of opinion on mixed demonstrations only served to distract and obscure the aims of the peace movement as a whole. The images of police dragging women away by their feet to vans and custody was powerfully disturbing. Once again, as with the images of the Ripper's victims, it was women's bodies on the ground, being manipulated by men.

By November I had put on nearly three stone, was permanently exhausted, and palpably unwell. My mother took me to the doctor. Could I have glandular fever? Would they test my thyroid function? A blood test was duly taken, the result, we were soon told, normal. I attempted to lose weight through a mixture of secretly purging in the bathroom after my midnight feasts and walking to school, instead of taking the bus. The route included Highcliffe Road, one of the steepest in Sheffield, a city composed of challenging hill starts. By the time I reached the top, I was purple in the face, and would lurch, sweating, into the common room, gasping for breath.

One December morning, at 5 a.m. – my mother away for the weekend and not informed of the excursion – Niamh and I boarded a minibus, hired by women, driven by women, filled with women – to Greenham. Our destination event was Reflect the Base, to mark a year since the first Embrace the Base demonstration. Following that occasion, in the early morning of New Year's Day 1983, forty-four women who had stayed on after the protest had broken through part of the perimeter fence to climb one of the silos inside the base, holding hands as they danced in a circle, until they were arrested, with thirty-six imprisoned. After this the police tactics had become harsher.

Inside the minibus the atmosphere in the pre-dawn cold and bluish dark was apprehensive and excited, a blur of noise: talking, exclaiming, singing, comparing exquisitely sewn banners and hastily assembled placards. My hessian bag contained a Tupperware box with Marmite sandwiches neatly cut into squares, a Penguin club biscuit (orange flavour), an apple, and three five-pound notes. Also, a personal item, as requested, to affix to the wire fence at the base. Niamh, a veteran of these expeditions, seemed to have brought only a flask of weak coffee. On instruction I was wearing gumboots, jeans over which I had tugged a pair of multicoloured striped leg warmers, an Aran jumper and the heaviest coat I could find from the many hung up in the hall at home. My hair was piled up underneath my astrakhan hat; on my hands, black fingerless wool gloves: I was aiming for anonymity.

A relatively pampered teenager, I was unprepared for the mud, the bleakness, or the dismal nature of the tents. People lived here? Perhaps it was more bearable in the summer. But what struck me more was the sense of optimism, collectiveness, and creativity; this was not the mania of a cult (I thought back to Katherine Mansfield at the Gurdjieff Institute). This was women subverting the traditional roles of homemaking for a purpose. For those in the damp tents, Greenham *was* their home. They were protecting it, as they were trying to protect the planet.

At the end of September, when boulders had been placed at the Yellow Gate to try and prevent women from camping there, the women simply incorporated the rocks into their living space, decorating them with banners as if they were part of the ruins of a city. Their Troy.

We were organising, we were massing, there was no sense of chaos, the energy was unstoppable. There were thousands of women here, of all ages: young, and old. Children, too. So many Cassandras. My mother should be with us, I realised. We had gone on a Books Against the Bomb march in London the year before. I wished I'd let her know what I was doing. Katherine Mansfield flashed into my mind again: *'It is intensely cold here.'* The situation was, as they say, fast-moving. We took up positions around the perimeter fence, its forbidding height similar to the high imprisoning wall of my old school. I had a small hand mirror in the pocket of my coat. We were to each hold a mirror up in silent vigil to give the base the opportunity to reflect back on itself and its potential for destruction. First, I attached my personal symbolic item to the fence: an old leather purse on a cord, in the shape of an owl, with buttons for eyes. The owl represented the Roman goddess Minerva, a symbol of wisdom, and courage, too. I would need some courage, for I had lost Niamh in the throng and confusion.

The silent vigil erupted into music, one of the popular Greenham songs: *'We are women/we are women/we are strong/we are strong'* to the tune of 'Frère Jacques'. Giant woollen woven spiderwebs, the Greenham talisman of strength and fragility, floated into view, and the voices carrying from all around the perimeter fence were as one, clear and hoarse, faint and steady.

We turned to face the lines of police. A sharp scent of woodsmoke emitted from the numerous campfires, glowing like beacons on an ancient shore. My clothes and hair would reek of it when I eventually returned home to Sheffield hours later, after parts of the fence had been torn down and hundreds of women arrested.

The air crackled with an emotion as strong as radio-activity. Above the noise of barking dogs, and the whining drone of a helicopter, came the unmistakable sound of a mistle thrush.

Christa Wolf, while standing in the ruins of the fortress where the captured Cassandra allegedly met her death, imagined the prophetess's last moments. They came to me now, my back to the impenetrable wire fence, as a symbol of defiance:

Here is the place. These stone lions looked at her.
They seem to move in the shifting light.

The furry moth which had been lodged in my throat all year began to unfurl, to release itself. Tears coursed down my cheeks.

I opened my mouth and began to sing.

Chapter Six

We Are the Dead

The clock struck midnight on New Year's Eve, and 1983 slid with studied indifference into the next year. I lay on the living-room floor, Bowie's *Diamond Dogs* on the record player, the needle pressed firmly into the groove of 'We Are the Dead', as I twitched with all the manic fervour of a cult leader poised for the rapture.

For months, primed by an over-literal reading of George Orwell's *1984*, I had been mentally preparing for this moment, when – surely! – a dystopian avalanche would descend all at once. I was unaware then that dystopias inch forward by mundane, if ever more outrageous, degrees.

And yet, the reality of the actual year of 1984 would, for many, more than live up to, perhaps even surpass, Orwellian fantasy.

Not long after New Year, I participated in a mass CND demo outside Sheffield City Hall. This time however, the protest was not real. The demo was staged – a scene in a film. The Bran Flakes, Rice Krispies and tomato ketchup with which my face was later smeared to simulate oozing wounds and burns were part of my costume, so too were the torn old clothes I wore for another scene, jerking and writhing on the ground. The film was called *Threads*.

Barry Hines, the film's writer, grew up in nearby Barnsley, the grandson of a coal miner. His best-known book, *A Kestrel for a Knave*, was adapted as the iconic film *Kes* in 1969, directed by Ken Loach. When I was twelve or thirteen *A Kestrel for a Knave*, with its local author, familiar landscape, and status as a modern classic, was put forward for study at school. Letters were duly dispatched to would-be flustered parents explaining that this was a book they might prefer their delicate middle-class daughters not to read, because of its 'brutal' (i.e. working class and poor) subject matter, its dialect (our own South Yorkshire dialect) and its liberal employment of 'shocking' sentences such as the wonderfully alliterative '*hands off cocks, on socks*'. Those girls – and there were a surprising number – whose parents forbade them from entering the fierce world of bullied Billy Casper and his beloved pet kestrel were condemned to sit in a separate class and sedately turn the pages of Thomas Hardy's *Under the Greenwood Tree*. My mother exasperatedly objected to any attempt at banning 'difficult' literature, pointing out that no one made a fuss about *Jane Eyre*, which we were also reading, and which is violent in the extreme. There seemed to be a convenient obliviousness to the fact that women also write about violence, as well as experience it.

Hines's new project was the story of a nuclear attack on Sheffield and the years that follow. Hines, and the director of *Threads*, Mick Jackson, were determined to show the true horror of the effects of nuclear war on an ordinary city and its population. This was no Hollywood film. It was crude, unforgettable and shockingly real. It was the first film shown on British television to fully depict a nuclear attack, and its aftermath. In 1966, *The War Game*, in a similar genre, had only been given a limited cinema release, the Wilson government fearing an epidemic of suicide among the UK population if it were to be aired more widely.

In May 1980, *Panorama* had shown the ludicrously inadequate but still terrifying *Protect and Survive* public information film. The government's propaganda response to global crisis was predictably clunky – no one of my generation would forget the later 1987 HIV/AIDS television advert featuring a giant tombstone imploring, in a highly melodramatic and yet utterly impersonal way, 'Don't Die of Ignorance'. *Threads* was intent on debunking the myth of methodical preparation which would in turn guarantee survival. Similar images to those used in the *Protect and Survive* film and on government-related leaflets – a giant mushroom cloud engulfing an outline of a conventional family (man, woman, two children, naturally) – were subverted to a chilling degree in *Threads*.

The choice of Sheffield as the location for *Threads* was deliberate. 'Britain's fourth-largest city, population 545,000' – as the film informs us through printed facts appearing over a backdrop of the famous cooling towers of the Tinsley Viaduct – was known to its inhabitants, bemused outsiders, and a frequently hostile press as the capital of the People's Republic of South Yorkshire. The original appellation came from a writer at the *Yorkshire Evening Post* but was readily adopted by the city's left-wing, socialist council.

Like Ken Livingstone's GLC in London, Sheffield City Council's ideology, with David Blunkett as leader, was far removed from that of Thatcherism. The council refused to set a budget in the rate-capping rebellion of 1985, a revolt led by mostly Labour-run English councils in an attempt to prevent Margaret Thatcher from withdrawing funds from local government. Transport was heavily subsidised – I never took a bus journey that cost more than five pence. And most relevantly here, South Yorkshire self-declared itself as an anti-nuclear, demilitarised zone. On May Day each year the red flag was hoisted above the town hall, and a peace treaty was exchanged with the city of Donetsk, Crimea, then part of Soviet Ukraine.

One of Sheffield's local newspapers – *The Star* – advertised for actors and extras to appear in *Threads*. Auditions took place at Sheffield City Hall ballroom. Over 1,000 people turned up. Extras were selected on the basis of height, age and the ability to look authentically depressed. I was a perfect match for the last requirement.

Threads was filmed in just over three weeks on a tiny budget of £250,000. The entire shoot took only seventeen days. The scenes with extras were episodic, a day or two at most.

The film opens with an image of a giant spider's web and a portentous voiceover informing viewers that '*everything connects*'. The spider's web was not dissimilar to the ones I had recently seen enveloping the tents at Greenham Common.

On the moors above Sheffield a young couple are making out in a car to the sound of Chuck Berry on the radio. Ruth is middle class, Jimmy working class; she becomes pregnant; their families meet. Hines wrote the characters as a symbol of Sheffield's class divide. The film, as well as tackling the reality of using nuclear weapons on civilians, is also a metaphor of the way Britain's working-class communities and industries were being pulverised by the Thatcher machine's vision of a free-market economy.

There are forty-six minutes of excruciating tension before the nuclear strike hits. People chat in a pub – The Nottingham House in Broomhill – while the latest tensions between the global superpowers are relayed over the television. A schoolgirl swigs milk from a pint bottle and turns to the radio. A lad runs to tell his mother that the Soviet Union and America have started a war. A woman involuntarily pees down her leg in fear. A cloud of gas floats above the city. And then comes the blast, somewhere between Debenhams and Woolworths on The Moor, a pedestrianised shopping area in the city centre.

Filming *Threads* was scary but exhilarating, with the false excitement of adrenaline and the real thrill of having a purpose. I felt a grim determination to play my part, a form of glum civic duty, doubtless exacerbated by the cold, the damp and the discomfort. As we extras marched

and suffered and died, lines from the First World War
poet Isaac Rosenberg, star of my English A-level syllabus,
played through my mind, like a mantra:

The air is loud with death,
The dark air spurts with fire,
The explosions ceaseless are.

Around me the atmosphere was surreal – the noise of early
warning sirens, screaming, a mess of confusion followed
by a deadly quiet, a stillness. Needless to say, I was not
one of the survivors.

Burnt black by strange decay
Their sinister faces lie.

The full impact of the film came with the completed
screening. While it horrified the audience who first saw
Threads on BBC2 on the evening of 24 September 1984
– for which over six million tuned in – the fact that this
was our city, our streets, our surrounding countryside had
an enduring impact. It was disturbing, and emotional. In
the film, prams are abandoned on The Moor and people
run scattergun in panic across Barker's Pool. The infamous
Egg Box building, built in 1977 as a modern extension to
Sheffield's Victorian town hall, is annihilated in the blast,
despite having been built to last 500 years.

After the nuclear strike, the film moves to the post-apoc-
alypse. These scenes were shot in the Peak District, some

six weeks after the main bulk of the film. By this time spring had arrived and fake snow had to be provided to mimic the appearance of a nuclear winter. The film's final, unforgettable image looks ahead presciently to imminent disasters like Chernobyl, just two years away, and the mutations and sickness which would be its awful legacy for future generations.

In Sheffield, winter – the real, not the nuclear variety – dripped into a cold, cloudy spring. I was undergoing my own, unsolicited, metamorphosis, which felt very much like a personal dystopia. I had gained nearly five stone in as many months. Dulled by extreme, enervating fatigue, my breathing had grown heavy and frustrated. Nights were delirious with the panic caused by a rapidly beating heart. Tiny armies marched through every joint and sinew, wading through my bloodstream, their miniature bayonets and sabres primed to assault frazzled nerve endings. As the dysmorphia reached its zenith, it was matched by over-consumption. I wanted – *needed* – to eat all the time. It seemed as if I would eat myself out of existence.

I grew forgetful, sleepy in class, unable to retain much information. One late afternoon at school, looking out of the window during triple French, I saw a black horse leaping and bounding across the stormy playing fields outside. Its unfettered wildness seemed to emphasise my embodied imprisonment; I turned back to my heavily underscored copy of Balzac's *Eugénie Grandet* and when I looked again the horse had gone.

That spring of 1984, the country, like me, seemed in the grip of dysmorphia, too. A malformation of the state.

On 23 March, Sarah Tisdall, a twenty-three-year-old junior civil servant at the Foreign and Commonwealth Office, was sentenced to six months in jail. The previous October, Tisdall had photocopied two classified documents relating to the date of arrival of the first US Cruise missiles at Greenham Common. The documents were delivered to the *Guardian*, which splashed an exclusive the weekend of 23 October 1983 to coincide with a major CND rally in London, the biggest single protest against nuclear weapons to date. 'I felt the public had a right to know what was being done to them,' Tisdall later said. Perhaps the most incriminating of the leaks was the report of the 'massive strengthening' of security at Greenham to coincide with the arrival of the missiles, and the resulting protests that might entail. During a particularly heated Prime Minister's Question Time on 1 November 1983, Labour MP Roland Boyes had asked the government for a guarantee that any protesters aiming to disrupt the base would not be shot; the then Secretary of State for Defence Michael Heseltine replied: 'I categorically will give no such assurance.' Against this alarming and volatile backdrop, it was unsurprising that I had told no one of my visit to Greenham the previous December.

On 21 March 1984, two days before Sarah Tisdall was sentenced to prison, and unconnected to the case, a retired elderly horticulturalist who specialised in growing roses was abducted from her home in Shrewsbury and driven away in her own car. Hilda Murrell was seventy-eight, a committed environmentalist, opposed to nuclear weapons and deeply concerned about the harm connected to the dumping of radioactive waste. Informed and independent, she had been due to deliver a paper that summer to the inquiry into a proposed new nuclear plant in Suffolk, the Sizewell B Pressurised Water Reactor. Three days after the abduction, Murrell was found murdered.

Almost immediately, conspiracy theories began to swarm. It was claimed that Murrell had been keeping documents in her house on behalf of her nephew, a senior naval intelligence officer during the recent Falklands War. These documents were rumoured to relate to classified security information about the contentious sinking of the Argentine cruiser the SS *Belgrano* on 2 May 1982, which led to the loss of 323 lives and the subsequent infamous utterance of Margaret Thatcher: 'Rejoice', memorably translated into 'Gotcha' on the front page of *The Sun* the next day.

The Tisdall and Murrell stories dominated the media throughout the spring of 1984. The shadowy, sinister involvement of the security services was all too believable: the dark apparatus of the state, unleashed against its more troublesome citizens, seemed to have stepped straight out of Orwell. These were ordinary women, more Cassandras going to extraordinary lengths to warn the public of potential catastrophe.

But even the urgency of the nuclear debate was about to be overshadowed. The 1984–85 miners' strike, though only lasting a year, would cauterise an entire industry, lead to a major subduing of unions' and workers' rights, and divide and impoverish working-class families and communities for decades. In Sheffield, South Yorkshire and Derbyshire, its events would play out right on our doorstep.

By 1984, Margaret Thatcher's government was five years into its remorseless grip on Britain, its dismantling of nationalised, public industries into private ownership well under way. By the early 1980s, one in five people was out of work, with the heaviest casualties in Northern Ireland and the industrial parts of Scotland and northern England. In 1984 the miners were striking not for wage increases but for their very livelihoods, for the viability of coal mining itself.

On 12 March 1984, Arthur Scargill, president of the National Union of Mineworkers (NUM), declared that strikes in local coalfields were to be escalated to a national level and called for strike action across the NUM membership. On 22 March it was announced that the strike was official, despite there being no overall vote. This lack of a national ballot played into the hands of the National Coal Board (NCB) and divided the mining community into strikers and 'scabs' (working miners). The 'scabs' crossed the strikers' picket lines to keep working. Meanwhile 'flying pickets' were posted to areas where the strike was weak.

The NUM's base was in the heart of Sheffield, at St James House on Vicar Lane near Sheffield Cathedral, a temporary headquarters while new offices were built next to the City Hall on Barker's Pool. Sheffield and South Yorkshire, then, became a focus for the chaos and torment which unfolded over the next year. In North Derbyshire only 67 per cent of miners were striking, dropping to 11 per cent in the south of the county – in contrast to parts of Yorkshire where 97 per cent of miners voted to strike.

In Sheffield and the local Labour party, opinion was divided about Scargill. According to who was asked, he was either a brilliant orator, charismatic, doughty, dogged, or unscrupulous, media-hungry and a bellowing finger-pointer. General sympathy lay with the striking miners and their families. Soon a 'Coal Not Dole' badge was added to the anti-nuclear symbols pinned to my schoolbag.

It was a bright cold day in April, and the clocks were striking thirteen.

On 12 April 1984, a tense stand-off took place between striking miners and police in Barker's Pool, outside Sheffield City Hall. The miners were lobbying the NUM executive conference taking place inside the organisation's headquarters, to protest the government's plans to force them into a secret ballot. They insisted that no miner had the right to vote another miner out of a job. After giving a typically bullish speech at the conference, Arthur Scargill used a megaphone to address the crowds from a balcony. Lines of police faced lines of miners. Lines of miners faced lines of police. This scenario would be repeated over and over again during the year that followed. Watching footage of the showdown, I was reminded of Greenham Common. This time, however, there was the unmistakable heat of maleness in confrontation with itself, eyeball to eyeball: the uniformed, helmeted police with batons, against the bareheaded miners in jeans, T-shirts and bomber jackets. The images on the television screen and in the newspapers were contemporary yet centuries old: men lining up, preparing for combat; but, just as with Greenham, it seemed clear that ultimately only one side would prevail in this 'civil war without guns' as the strike was later described.

That stasis, that civil war, was in me too. A few days after the Barker's Pool face-off, my sister took me to see the family GP. It was almost Easter. The weather was warm; the lime trees lining the street outside newly in leaf.

Even though my sister was six months pregnant, by this time I was heavier than she was. My inexplicable and rapid weight gain was reported to the GP, a socially awkward woman of about thirty. Her eyes slid over me incuriously then looked away. 'Could it be puppy fat?' she asked.

'I'm not a *dog*,' I protested.

'Could she be pregnant?'

My sister looked scandalised. 'Certainly not!'

I turned on her in indignation. 'How do *you* know?' But of course, I couldn't be pregnant, I had never even had sex.

My sister reminded the GP that I had had some blood tests six months before, in October. It was the other doctor at the practice who had ordered the tests and conveyed the results, which had been, we were told, normal. Clearly bored, the GP flicked through the notes in my file. When she came to the relevant page she stopped, slammed the folder shut, reached for a script and after quickly writing something down handed it to my sister. Her manner had changed; it was now brisk and professional. 'I'd like to have those tests run again,' she said. 'Today, if possible.'

At the Hallamshire hospital, the blood, dark ruby-red, was sucked out of a vein in my left arm and into several vampiric test tubes.

A few days later. Thursday. The following day was Good Friday. At about 6 p.m., the letterbox slammed. Looking out of the living-room window, I saw the GP skittering down our thirteen front steps. Slowly, I opened the door that divided the hall from the front porch. After picking up the sealed note on the mat and reading its contents, I passed into a different world, one never completely left since that early evening in April 1984 – the world of the chronically unwell.

Your blood tests are abnormal.

(The dictionary definition of abnormal: *defective, unusual, deviant.*)

No further information apart from an appointment time for the following Tuesday at 9 a.m., and '*Please bring your parent or guardian with you.*' That gave me five days – the entire Easter long weekend – to speculate about which terminal illness I might have.

My mother and I faced the doctor together on Tuesday morning at the appointed time. The GP did not look at me directly. Apparently, the blood tests had indicated my thyroid levels were '*dangerously*' – she cleared her throat, correcting herself to the slightly less alarming '*very*' – high. She had urgently referred me to an endocrinology consultant at the Hallamshire.

I wished I had listened more in Biology. My knowledge of what the thyroid was and where it lurked was vague. A gland at the front of the neck, which in my case had been swelling for months and causing weight gain and drastic changes to my metabolism. My mother had always used iodised salt in cooking as a prevention for this as my father and one of his sisters had had thyroid issues. In fact, that sister had died aged twenty-one following a thyroid operation, but as with most family stories I had only half listened. Now, in the consulting room, I became vigilant.

My mother queried the previous tests of six months before. The GP flushed, all the way up from her neck to her face, her skin exactly the colour of the pink latex washing-up gloves kept under our kitchen sink.

'I'm very sorry. The results were missed.'

A short silence, and then my mother asked me to wait for her outside. Closing the door to the consulting room behind me, away from the suddenly sharply raised voices, I left the surgery.

In a few days I would turn seventeen.

In the last six months I had finally achieved what nine years at my previous school had failed to deliver:

actual, not fair-weather friends; a social life. University seemed probable. This new sense of possibility within my own life was amplified by what was going on around me. By the mid-80s, the provinces were beginning to feel the influence of the Blitz Club in London, the venue that had spawned the New Romantic scene and launched the careers of Spandau Ballet, Boy George, Marilyn, and Siobhan Fahey of Bananarama among others. *i-D* magazine, set up in 1980 by former *Vogue* art director Terry Jones, focused on street style and youth culture – and crucially, that culture was not confined to London. In the December 1984/January 1985 issue of *i-D*, two regular attendees at Sheffield's The Limit club were photographed and featured, a status my friends and I yearned to achieve. These particular young women would, they told *i-D*, 'give it all up for punk'. The same issue of *i-D* featured the top ten tracks currently played at the club.

The Limit was a teenage rite of passage; I first descended its squelchy stairs in the autumn of 1983 just as my brothers had, years before. It was my turn now. *History is made at night.* History is made in pubs and in clubs, in record stores and on dance floors. Sheffield was a city in which there was proximity to celebrity. Every afternoon after school, my route home took me past the house on Ringinglow Road in which Sheffield's most famous pop group, The Human League, were rumoured to all live together. Two classic motorbikes were always parked on the forecourt. Anything was possible, I thought.

This mysterious energy-sapping illness, this new bulk of a body, like the proverbial thief in the night, seemed intent on destroying any sense of choice. While we still gathered at each other's houses to watch *Brookside*, *The Young Ones* or *The Tube* on TV, I was, by that spring, too tired to do much more. I no longer accompanied Natalie to The Limit on Fridays, or to Sin Bin at TurnUps on Commercial Street for 70s classics on Wednesday evenings (£1 on the door).

When I had told one of my friends about the doctor's appointment, the response had been, jokingly, 'They'd better find something wrong with you, otherwise you're just being really boring.' The comment stuck. Anything was better than *boring*. Even illness.

My mother emerged from the GP surgery just as an ice-cream van – impossibly early for the day – trundled into view across from us. Her face showed its familiar mix of preoccupation and determination. The van hopefully blared out its familiar tune of 'Greensleeves'. I was, as usual, starving, despite wolfing down four slices of heavily buttered toast before leaving home.

We walked slowly back to our house, licking our ice-cream cones.

The consultant, Dr F—, with whom we were granted an audience, was jolly, affable and enthusiastic. He rubbed his hands together as he pronounced me *atypical* – a word which I knew meant the same as *abnormal*. He explained that I had Graves' disease, an auto-immune condition causing hyperthyroidism.

Had I heard of Graves' disease?

'Yes,' I answered, surprising myself. 'Christina Rossetti had it.'

'She reads a lot of poetry,' my mother explained, parenthetically.

The thyroid, Dr F— explained further, is a small, butterfly-shaped gland at the front of the neck which controls the body's entire metabolism, bones, growth and sexual development, even though it weighs less than twenty-eight grams. Mine was overworking, producing too many thyroid hormones, but unusually for hyperthyroidism, which increases the appetite while causing weight loss, the reverse had happened and I had gained weight. Lots of weight. Hence *atypical*.

Dr F— asked me to hold out my hands. To his satisfaction, there was a slight tremor. He bombarded me with questions, about my skin, was it dry, and rough? My eyes – were they sore, gritty? Did my muscles feel weak? Was I constipated, or the opposite? Were my periods regular? I squirmed uncomfortably in my chair. Then Dr F— walked round to the back of the chair, encircled my neck with both his hands and asked me to swallow – an unpleasant ritual that would be repeated over the weeks, months and years, whenever I had a consultation about my thyroid, and which I came to dread. I would still feel a choking sensation for days afterwards. '*A nice little goitre*,' he pronounced, sitting back down behind his desk, opposite me and my mother.

Dr F— prescribed carbimazole, a medicine in tablet form, which I was to take every day, three times a day, for the foreseeable; I would be required to attend the clinic, on a weekly basis at first, for blood tests. Before he dismissed us, Dr F— cheerily urged me not to be anxious. 'Have you seen the film *Dr Strangelove*?' I confessed that I had not. He went on to add that the film's subtitle was *How I Learned to Stop Worrying and Love the Bomb*.

'That's what I want you to do – stop worrying and love the bomb!'

My parallel life began. Each week I would attend the endocrinology clinic as its youngest patient. In the waiting room the spectre of what might happen to my *'nice little goitre'* was displayed before me. Many of the older patients had much more advanced symptoms. This type of enlarged goitre was still known locally as 'Derbyshire neck' thanks to endemic iodine deficiency in the soil and water of the Peak District over two centuries, although it had much improved by the 1980s. The historical neurological deficiencies which accompanied the untreated goitre were well documented. I tried not to stare at these men and women who appeared as if from another century with their disproportionately swollen necks like a permanent surgical brace composed of a huge lump of additional flesh, which caused extreme shortness of breath, hoarseness and difficulty swallowing.

Dr F— seemed pleased with my progress. After about three weeks from starting the carbimazole, some of my symptoms were decreasing and – to my enormous relief – I was beginning to lose weight, which was all I really cared about. As I held out my hands straight in front of me as required on every visit, he would shout 'Steady as a rock!' as if I were a horse about to head out from the starting block, waiting for Dr F— to fire the gun.

The excess weight dropped off at the rate of approximately four pounds a week; my appetite was suppressed by the tablets. By the end of the summer, I had lost over four stone. I stopped wheezing and my heartbeat returned to normal. Like Alice in Wonderland, I had found my own magic toadstool in the form of carbimazole, with Dr F— the hookah-smoking Caterpillar controlling the proceedings. He determined which parts of the mushroom I would eat, and when.

In purely formulaic terms Dr F— saved my life. But it was not without consequences. A year of radical weight gain and loss left its imprint on my body. The medication caused ferocious side effects, the worst being muscle spasms and savage skin rashes in the form of itchy pustules. As the flesh decreased, its rapid departure bequeathed a map of stretch marks, crisscrossing the backs of my knees, under my arms, beneath my breasts, and on my hips, impressions similar to the silver trails left by slugs on the back doorstep on summer mornings. I despaired that this body would ever be looked at by anyone other than me, that it would ever be found desirable. I had also missed a great deal of school.

While my body underwent its discombobulating inner and outer transformation, the body politic was experiencing a more serious convulsion.

Close to home, near Rotherham in South Yorkshire, the Orgreave Coking Plant was the scene of a bloody, sustained fight between striking miners and police on 18 June 1984, known subsequently as The Battle of Orgreave.

On a hot, sunny day in midsummer, three months into the strike, the sound of skylarks high overhead was drowned out by the roar of police, carrying riot shields and mounted on horseback, charging towards miners who had answered Arthur Scargill's call to picket the coking plant en masse in order to block lorries leaving Orgreave. What followed was among the worst examples of police violence in dealing with industrial unrest ever witnessed in modern times.

The pickets had made their way to Orgreave in cars and coaches, finding their journey mysteriously easy at a time when roadblocks were regularly set up to thwart their progress. When they arrived, police even helped them find places to park. But after the final lorry drove away from Orgreave, the miners were set upon in a systematic fashion, even as they relaxed after their picket, buying food from a local branch of Asda, lolling on the grass. An ice-cream van idled in the background. Some eight thousand pickets were at the scene and approximately five thousand police officers. Over three hundred police were wearing riot gear – the first time riot police had ever been deployed on the British mainland.

The 'official' story, insisted on later by Margaret Thatcher and by complicit media such as *The Sun*, was that the pickets had been throwing stones and the police had had no choice but to charge. However, what the public saw – including me, who like millions watched the television news later that day – confirmed the opposite. What we saw were police on horseback galloping into a defenceless crowd. We saw men, and some women, beaten viciously; led away with blood streaming down their faces and bodies; trying to escape across a nearby railway line; pinned to the ground and overwhelmed. We saw police injured too.

After Orgreave, a total of ninety-five people were charged, variously, with riot, unlawful assembly and violent disorder. At the time, a conviction for rioting could lead to a sentence of life imprisonment. All the cases were dropped, in the light of questions about the unreliability of police evidence. Many of the officers' statements were oddly similar, strangely replicated. According to a BBC report, 'A miner accused of throwing a stone had actually been photographed holding a pork pie.'

The group Women Against Pit Closures had, by the time of Orgreave, become a cornerstone of the Miners' Strike. Women Against Pit Closures was formed in Barnsley by a collective led by Betty Cook, known as 'Queen of Coal', and soon other branches sprang up across the country. Rather like Greenham, the WAPC groups were a mixture. Those involved were mainly working-class women from coalfield communities, but there were also women's liberation activists and local people who just wanted to help, such as my mother.

The WAPC organised soup kitchens, fundraised, held rallies, and adopted some of the tactics used at Greenham. Sit-ins were held at mineshafts. Miners' pit lamps were sent countrywide as symbols of inspiration. As with Greenham, for many women this was their first taste of activism, and empowerment. Some of this, more often than not, clashed with the more traditionally held views of the miners themselves. Women were suitable to run a soup kitchen, but picketing and demonstrating were another matter. Men were the breadwinners, and the communities were focused – as they had been for generations – on an ethos of masculinity, of supporting those who worked in what was one of the most dangerous jobs in any industry. This attitude was not just specific to mining areas. It was still the early 1980s. The very idea of women's liberation, other than in limited ways, was generally considered with utter suspicion and often contempt by the wider public, institutions, and the media – and also the very trade unions that promulgated ideas of equality.

Our perceived inferiority was inculcated.

1984 was not the first time Sheffield and its environs had seen widely reported direct action. The notorious Sheffield Outrages were a series of explosions and murders by trade union militants which took place in the city in the mid-1860s, as a result of a Grinders' Union strike protesting about insufficient wages and lack of safeguarding from employers on introducing new machinery.

The Outrages became known in local folklore as The Stirrings.

In 1843, the average age of mortality in Sheffield was just twenty-four years. A contemporary postcard from the mid-century portrays a city of chimneys and furnaces belching soot and smoke, engulfing cramped and insanitary housing. Its title? 'On a Very Clear Day'.

The Outrages were immortalised as *The Stirrings in Sheffield on Saturday Night!*, a musical documentary written by local playwright Allen Cullen, with music by Roderick Horn, which premiered at the Sheffield Playhouse in Temperance Hall in May 1966, a century after the original Grinders' Union strike. In 1973, *The Stirrings* was revived at the newly opened Crucible Theatre, the successor to The Playhouse, round the corner in Norfolk Street. My parents were in the audience; the record of the musical's widely popular soundtrack was regularly played at home.

Ironically, given its etymology, The Stirrings was also the name of a posh restaurant on Oakbrook Road at Nether Green, at the bottom of Hangingwater Road. Its bulbous, billowing glass frontage was opaque, with the restaurant's name imprinted in Stymie Black Italic – the classic 1970s font. I never saw anyone going in or out of The Stirrings, which was rumoured to be the most expensive place to eat in Sheffield. On only two momentous occasions, very close together in 1978, would I enter this hallowed place. The first was for my sister's wedding lunch that March, when we were served duck and Black Forest gateau. The second was my eldest brother's twenty-first birthday in July; exactly the same menu was offered. My overriding memory of that event was of my brother and his best friend, unfamiliarly and handsomely suited, striking matches off the soles of their polished shoes to light their cigarettes. This flamboyant gesture deeply impressed me; I begged to be shown how to do it myself.

That summer of 1984 was a busy one, even for someone as obviously unwell as I still was. Hospital visits, blood tests, rattling buckets for donations for the WAPC, working in the bookshop, listening to the velvet-green lushness of Prefab Sprout's debut album *Swoon* and the spiky anger of Elvis Costello's *Punch the Clock*, and sleeping a lot. Alone, I would sit and read books in the café at the top of the Graves Art Gallery in the Art Deco Central Library on Surrey Street. In the gallery itself, I was constantly drawn to one painting in particular – Gwen John's *A Corner of the Artist's Room in Paris, 1907–1909*. This work, of which John would paint many versions, seems, with its muted colours and sparse objects, to be simplicity itself. A wicker armchair is positioned next to a low wooden table underneath a window, the view from which can only just be discerned. The light is grey. It is perhaps a morning in very early spring. The wall behind the chair, onto which has been flung a blue dress or wrapper and against which rests a white parasol, is a deep yellow. More than anything, the room announces the presence of its inhabitant even though she is not there. It was painted in John's attic room in an eighteenth-century house at 87 rue du Cherche-Midi in Montparnasse. I wanted to live in the solitude of that room, to be that self. It unfolded before me like a story.

At school, my friendships with Natalie and Fay solidified. Often I'd spend nights staying over on one or the other's bedroom floor – their houses were round the corner from each other in Bents Green. We'd hang out at the Hammer and Pincers, the 'school pub' on Ringinglow Road. For sophistication, we had Mr Kite's bistro on Division Street with its memorably insipid coffee served with UHT milk. We went along to the gigs of a not especially successful local band called Pulp, because the lead singer Jarvis Cocker's cousin was in our year.

Autumn brought a sharp reckoning, as the evenings snatched themselves in, pinched and mean, and the days grew colder. Even as Scargill ended most of his speeches with the rallying cry '*the miners united will never be defeated*' there remained the salient fact that the miners were *not* united about strike action, especially in the Nottinghamshire and Midland coalfield areas closest to Sheffield. After the trauma of Orgreave many miners had gone back to work. This was the era personified by the character of Yosser Hughes in the 1982 TV series *Boys from the Blackstuff*, played by actor Bernard Hill, who was himself from a mining family. Hughes is a working-class Liverpool hard man brought down by unemployment and despair. His catchphrases 'Gizza job' and 'I can do that' became an integral part of the economic misery of the early 1980s.

As autumn deepened into winter, music came out to support the miners. We paid 50p to see Billy Bragg do a benefit gig at Sheffield City Hall – Bragg's record 'Between the Wars', released in February 1985, became one of the anthems of the strike and haunted its final months.

At school, another insurrection was advancing – in the form of a play. Our teachers took the bold step of entrusting the sixth form and fifth years with a production of Bertolt Brecht and Kurt Weill's *The Threepenny Opera*, to be performed in December, just before the Christmas holidays. The 'play with music' as Brecht termed it, was first performed in Berlin at the end of August 1928. In 1933, when the Nazis came to power, Weill and Brecht both fled Germany for the United States. In Sheffield in late 1984, there was no better expression of the times than to put on a socialist play which skewered capitalist society. Brecht and Weill were synonymous with the cultural innovations of the Weimar Republic. *The Threepenny Opera* was an immediate hit when it opened. In it, Brecht portrays the German bourgeoisie sticking two fingers up at high society, with the anti-hero Macheath, known as Mack the Knife, presiding, like a sleek, self-satisfied cat, over a cast of pimps and sex workers. Capitalism corrupts, is the play's pro-Marxist theme. 'Food is the first thing: morals follow on.' Weill's off-kilter songs, based on German dance tunes, are delivered in 'rough style'; these undoubtedly made the play the success it continues to be.

It was a giddy three months as we prepared the production. Between October and December 1984, romances and enmities flourished equally.

The Threepenny Opera's songs remain in my head, as if implanted. During that winter, I jiggled my small nephew, the newest addition to our family, to inappropriate and graphic alternative lullabies like 'The Ballad of Sexual Dependency', or 'Liebeslied' ('Moon over Soho'). '*Mankind is kept alive by bestial acts*' I would sternly intone, just to watch his little face break into giggles.

Almost all my friends took part in the play, depicting a colourful assortment of so-called whores, beggars and thieves. I had wanted to act, but my illness and its concomitant exhaustion got in the way. Instead I became immersed on the production side, as the English teacher and play's director Mr V——'s assistant. Mr V—— was a wiry, energetic and passionate teacher, who was progressive in his diversity of casting and communication of ideas years before many theatres and film sets found it fashionable or requisite to be so. He encouraged us all to call him by his first name but we stuck with Mr V——.

During rehearsals, sharing the lemon curd sandwiches he'd brought from home, I made friends with Robbie, who was playing one of the beggars, I began spending time at his house with him and his older brother Julian. Regardless of the weather, Julian and I would sit on the back step, smoking roll-ups and drinking Guinness from cans, Bowie's *Hunky Dory* playing in the background. Julian never appeared anywhere, whatever the time of day or night, without a four-pack. This companionable rapport with boys was a new, welcome aspect to my sixth-form years. My brothers and their friends – indeed most of the men I came into contact with – were much older than me, and I hardly knew any boys of my own age. My only romance, when I was nearly fourteen, had petered out when the boy in question returned with his family to New Zealand. To see a boy as a friend, rather than a potential conquest, was revelatory.

Parallel to this, and paradoxically, part of me stayed remote and shut off. I dreamt of a silent life, as a type of anchorite. Precociously, I longed to withdraw from society in a vaguely ascetic way, although I had no religious beliefs. A nervous, stubborn instinct encouraged me towards a centrality of self quite separate from conventional expectation, to engage with reading, writing, and little else. The world and its endless horrors and cares seemed too much to bother about. Conversely, I remained desperate for immersion, but illness had made me look in, not out.

Around the time that *The Threepenny Opera* went into final rehearsals, in early December, I was surprised to discover I had a crush on a friend. I knew Conor mainly because our lockers were next to each other in the sixth-form common room, and we walked the same way home from school, usually with Robbie. We'd saunter down through Greystones to Ringinglow Road and part at Banner Cross: Robbie and Conor went the rest of the way together; their houses were off Psalter Lane, near

Chelsea Park. I would continue on to Ecclesall Road and Hunter's Bar. Conor and I both occupied a kind of no-man's land in the common room, an uneasy truce between two different and distinct groups: 'the trendies' and 'the boffins'. Conor had a place at Cambridge so was definitely a boffin, but he moved more easily between the different registers and hierarchies of the sixth form probably because he wasn't obsessed with them as I was. He had a fairly prominent role in the play, but didn't take it that seriously.

Up until this point, my sexual impulses had been sublimated. Clothes were selected not to attract attention, but worn as a means of disguise. The year before they had been too tight; now those same clothes were baggy and oversized. I shrank into them for safekeeping, feeling like a hundred-year-old waif rather than a girl of seventeen. Despite the sexual timidity, my imagination in this area was prolific: I listened to Prince's graphic and gorgeously filthy 'The Beautiful Ones' and 'Darling Nikki' from the *Purple Rain* album, over and over. *The Company of Wolves*, Neil Jordan's film of Angela Carter's short-story collection *The Bloody Chamber*, came out late in September 1984 with a screenplay by the author. The very obvious theme of sexual awakening, amid the nightmarish fantasy trope of Little Red Riding Hood alone in a dark forest, was irresistible.

As rehearsals turned into opening night, I longed to convey how I felt to Conor, but at that age traditional ideas about how men and women were supposed to interact were too ingrained. The early teenage diet of magazines like *Jackie* remained inherent: it wasn't up to me to make the first move, despite my subsequent self-education in contemporary feminist literature.

The Threepenny Opera was a resounding if uneven success. It ran for four nights. On the last night, the stage lights dimmed for the final time as the half-sung, half-spoken final couplet was uttered '*Those you see are in the daylight / Those in darkness don't get seen.*' Then all went black. I shivered at the potency of the words in a time when the miners who were still out on strike were freezing on the picket lines, and there were food parcels and collections under way to ensure their children could celebrate Christmas. In Ethiopia, reported by BBC News in late October, a famine of untold proportions had been described as 'the closest thing to hell on Earth', prompting Bob Geldof of The Boomtown Rats and Midge Ure of Ultravox to put together a supergroup of British and Irish musicians to record the charity hit single 'Do They Know It's Christmas'. The song was dreadful, but we had all bought the record.

Somewhat unwisely, Mr V— had offered to host the post-*Threepenny Opera* cast and crew party at his home. Everyone was on a high, some literally. Sitting next to Julian on the living-room floor, I accepted a glass of whisky. By midnight, Julian was grinding out cigarettes on Mr V—'s carpet and various cast members were getting better acquainted with each other, in non-verbal ways. Tonight was surely an opportunity for something

– as yet unimagined – to happen with Conor, but I hadn't seen him since we arrived at Mr V—'s. There were shapes outside, in the back garden, through the window, but the glass was steamed up; impossible to make them out. It was beginning to snow; by the time we left the party, the road and vehicles were gently frosted, a delicate sifting of icing sugar through a sieve. I was going home with Natalie. Her father had come to collect us. Fumbling with the car door, I spotted Conor for the first time in hours, his back turned to me, firmly holding the hand of a girl I had never seen before. I sobbed for what remained of the night on Natalie's bedroom floor while Frankie Goes to Hollywood's 'The Power of Love' mocked me from the stereo. *The Threepenny Opera*'s run had ended in professional triumph: personally, I was vanquished.

On New Year's Day 1985, I lay on a bed at the Hallamshire hospital, undergoing a nuclear thyroid scan. A radiopharmaceutical called a 'tracer' was injected into a vein in my left arm, which entered the thyroid gland via the circulating blood. Once inside the body, the tracer released gamma rays. Outside the body, a gamma scanner tracked the tracer and measured how the thyroid processed the radioactive iodine. All my convictions about the dangers of the nuclear industry and now I had its energy inside me! What a hypocrite.

In the long term, I wasn't getting better, despite the reduction in dosage of carbimazole tablets.

My body felt like a giant Geiger counter, although the risk was small, allegedly. I thought about the experience again later that year when the eco-thriller *Edge of Darkness* was shown on television. A widowed police detective, played by a world-weary Bob Peck, sets out to uncover the truth behind his environmental activist daughter's murder after she is shot to death in front of him, stumbling, as you do, on an international nuclear espionage conspiracy with the British government at its centre. The series was shown just a few months before the Chernobyl catastrophe occurred.

On 3 March 1985, the miners officially called off their strike. It had been a bitter, brutal year. Two days later the miners of Grimethorpe Colliery, South Yorkshire, went back to work accompanied by a brass band, little knowing that within seven years their pit would be closed for good. Ultimately, an entire industry would be destroyed with nothing to replace it, no more jobs for life or stable communities, and an end to a culture and identity that extended far beyond the coalfields. Unemployment would be driven up in all the ex-coalfield areas across Britain. In 2014, declassified documents indicated that in 1984 Thatcher had mooted the unprecedented idea of placing the UK under a state of emergency if the strike had continued. The last deep coal mine, Kellingley in North Yorkshire, was closed in 2015. In early 2023, to much protest and legal action in the face of the harm it would do to the environment, the Conservative government approved the creation of a new coal mine in Cumbria.

Under the spreading chestnut tree, I sold you, and you sold me.

It was early May, and the garden wall was warm to the touch once more. I was in hospital. Tomorrow I would be having my throat cut.

A necessary act of violence, so the surgeon told me.

Dr F— had announced that the medication I was taking wouldn't work for ever and that an operation to remove most or even all of my thyroid gland was needed. Mindful of the aunt who thirty years earlier had gone into hospital and never come out, I had resisted stubbornly. Now the surgeon had made it clear that if I didn't agree to a thyroidectomy, I would be subject to infertility and lifelong heart problems. I was still very young, he pointed out, gloomily.

At the Hallamshire, I had my own room, by luck rather than design. Earlier I had said goodbye to my mother and sister; I would see them when/if I woke up after the operation. I was erring more on the side of *if* than *when*. To distract myself, I switched on the television. An adaptation of Dorothy L. Sayers's novel *Have His Carcase* was under way. The story centres around the body of a man with a slit throat. I switched the television off.

The next morning, very early, they came to prepare me for the operation. I was naked underneath my hospital gown. A sacrifice. I panicked. '*I want to go home,*' I told the surgeon, emphatically. When the first injection of the pre-med hit, I ran screaming down the corridor and had to be led back to bed. Then, by degrees, I slipped under the anaesthetic.

As it happened my concerns were not irrational. I very nearly didn't make it back. When I awoke I was lying on what I first took to be a mortuary slab. '*I was right,*' I thought. It was freezing in this place, wherever it was. Figures in uniforms and masks were gliding around me. A strange man was rubbing my bare bottom, a woman my feet. I could not breathe. I tried to impart this vital information, but as I could not breathe nothing came out of my mouth. I shut my eyes again.

Later. Unbelievably, I was being hauled like a puppet into a sitting position. Daylight smacked against my eyelids. I opened my eyes, slowly, cautiously. I was in a bed, with screens around me, anxious faces, arms holding me up. A plastic sheet like an enormous baby's bib over my neck and chest, and tubes everywhere, one halfway into my neck. The oxygen mask was lifted off. A nurse hovered over me with a comb. 'Do you have a middle or a side parting?'

'A fringe,' I managed to gasp out, before vomiting over myself, the nurse, and the bed.

Later still. I woke again, this time to the faces of my mother and my sister. Not dead after all, then. They looked exhausted. I managed a weak smile. Apparently, I had 'panicked under the anaesthetic', not coming round for over four hours after the operation. They couldn't wake me up.

158

In fact, I didn't panic under the anaesthetic. I suffered a severe allergic reaction to the anaesthetic and went into respiratory paralysis. One of the side effects of this reaction is the inability to communicate while being conscious. This wouldn't be worked out for several years, when it was discovered that I have a rare blood plasma abnormality. Atypical, once again.

After I left hospital, I recuperated for five long weeks at my sister's house in Broomhall. The bookshop having closed for good the year before, our own house had been sold and my mother was now working in London. It was early summer. All I could see from the window was the dense green of the trees, and the wide night sky. I didn't sleep much. The pain from the wound in my neck was immense, the only relief the two paracetamol tablets allowed every four hours. Nothing stronger. When the tarpaulin came off, the slash across my throat looked ugly and serrated, like a jagged red ribbon, or, as someone commented, 'a scene from *Macbeth*'. I couldn't bear to look at it. Revolted, I neglected to clean my neck and tiny growths appeared around the edges of the scar. Miniature limpets attaching themselves to my skin. I picked them off, impatient and repulsed.

My mother visited every weekend. And at around six each morning, my nephew, now aged almost three, would push open the door to my room. 'Would you like a cup of tea?' came the polite enquiry; a small, serious butler. 'Yes please.' He would nod sagaciously and trot back to his bed, to fall asleep again.

Most of the time, I was alone. With only a cassette player for company, I marked the nights through the phases of the moon. Three tapes played in succession: Suzanne Vega, *Solitude Standing*, Prince, *Sign O' the Times*, and Simon and Garfunkel's *Sounds of Silence*.

Look at the Moon over Soho! I whispered to myself, my favourite line from *The Threepenny Opera*. I could almost track the path to the future by the few stars left in the sky as dawn approached.

Chapter Seven

Milk Teeth

Halfway through the Second Summer of Love, I lost my last milk tooth. It fell into the mouth of a stranger I'd been kissing in one of the fetid nightclubs I frequented, a baby incisor mistaken for a Disco Biscuit among a crowd forever freeze-framed in a shared MDMA moment of absolute euphoria. The sour smell of vomit, piss and cheap lager mingled with the iron reek of blood blooming from the wrists of a girl I encountered in the toilets, opening up her unhappy veins to yet another sticky-black Saturday night. 'Destroy the Heart' we sang in unison, me with a new gap in my smiley face.

On Saturday nights I was unconcerned about the week ahead. Sundays were for sleeping all day, only surfacing for family dinner, trying to disguise teeth chattering from the comedown. Mondays were spent back at my summer job in the cutlery factory for 8 a.m., packing knives into the waiting knife blocks which roamed the conveyor belt, my precarious pile growing higher and higher, glinting in the sun's arrival through tiny, implacable windows.

For now, it was still Saturday. It was Sheffield, August 1989. The Limit on West Street, the scene of my earliest forays into clubland, remained a legend in the city and beyond. In its basement the B52s made their first ever UK appearance, Joy Division had played a seminal set a decade earlier and, it was rumoured, Pink Floyd had once turned up for a surprise gig, but it was to remain open for only another eighteen months. We were making the most of it, but we knew its time had passed – The Leadmill, the new, smarter music venue near the railway station, was the place to be seen now, Primal Scream bawling out 'Ivy Ivy Ivy' the summer before we became the *Screamadelica* generation.

One night at the Leadmill, with a sick shock, I glimpsed my ex-boyfriend Daniel among the cool crowd, unmet for almost a year. We had lost our virginity to each other – or so we both assumed at the time – on an icy November afternoon, halfway through The Beatles' 'Savoy Truffle', track 3 of side 4 of *The White Album*. I'd hoped we'd make it as far as 'Revolution 9', but it was over very quickly. 'I think we're done,' he muttered, after brief and jabbing congress which lasted all of a minute. The following April he gave me a tambourine for my birthday then almost immediately dumped me for someone who smiled more readily than I did. Possessing little imagination, Daniel would regularly take her to 'our' place, the city's botanical gardens, where as a child I'd passionately kissed the cold face of the statue of Pan and as a teenager planned my escapade to Greenham Common. I spent the unhappy, dull weeks after my A-level exams spotting the two of them in the distance, looming menacingly over the pristine lawns.

That autumn I had fled as far away as possible – to university in Cardiff – returning at the end of the summer term with agonising sunburn from days spent swimming in a heatwave off the nearby Gower coast and an even more painful overdraft. Robbie, my closest friend at this time, had decamped to a villa in Portugal with a group he'd met at Cambridge. We were splitting, splintering apart. During that first year of university, I had visited him sporadically, getting the coach from Cardiff – an interminable 200 miles and six hours – bleary-eyed from drinking, dancing and occasionally studying, to enter a closed world of ancient privilege and teeth-grinding preciousness. At first our friendship – *contra mundum* – had continued much as it had in Sheffield. We'd hide away in his college rooms during the short winter days, earnestly reading poetry aloud, listening to Everything but the Girl and Tracy Chapman on tape. Our faces would move gradually closer to each other as the long night settled in behind the inevitable mullioned windows, until there was no space at all between us except the suddenly charged air. Eventually we would fall asleep sweatily entwined in his single bed. Sometimes we would abandon our twin solitude and emerge for an awkward evening with his friends, bright, friendly and curious about our undeclared relationship, and I would become defensive over my lack of Oxbridgeness and long for Cardiff: for Welsh accents, staggering out of Clwb Ifor Bach in the whitish dawn, the meticulously prepared pre-evenings getting plastered on Thunderbird and the half-savage, half-listless hunt for anyone, anyone at all.

The sweltering Sheffield summer was a continuation of this aimless search, albeit with added pressure to address my lack of money until my next student grant appeared in October. I was eligible for the full grant, due to my parents' divorced status. There was little temporary work on offer in Sheffield; I claimed there was none at all. My mother knew better and circled the few job ads in the local paper, which is how, a couple of weeks later, I ended up meeting Karen, Helen, and Giulia that first morning in the cutlery factory just past Bramall Lane. Temps clocking in among the regulars for our inaugural, inept shift, we fell upon each other like the co-conspirators we would become. The hours were long, the pay – topped up by an optional morning shift at double-time on Saturdays – seemed hard earned. The factory was unbearably hot, stinking of tar and metal. The sanitary bins in the toilets overflowed; flies buzzed ominously around the stale blood. The one non-white worker, an Asian woman in her thirties who didn't speak much English, was the target of relentless 'teasing' from the others, as, occasionally, was Giulia, who was Italian, but the permanent workers mostly kept away from us; we were students, 'clever' people playacting at real work. That first morning I cut my finger deeply on a serrated knife edge, fainted, and was sent off for a tetanus jab. But I became accustomed to it, the rhythm and the half-light, the stewed, bronze-coloured tea in the makeshift canteen, the crackling pages of *The Sun*, the endless smoking and swearing, the crisp £10 notes in a brown envelope at the end of each week.

There was an endlessness to the days that summer. I had little thought of the new, fierce friendships made over the previous year at Cardiff, or the rambling house in which I would set up home with seven other students at the beginning of the coming autumn term. For once, Sheffield, the city I had for years longed to leave behind, was the exact place I wanted to be, a city the very fibres of which seemed part of me as never before.

Sheffield in 1989 had shaken off neither the shackles of recession nor the tension between citizen and state. Four months earlier, I had been home for the Easter holidays, travelling by train from Cambridge, where I'd made a long detour to visit Robbie. It was a Saturday, 15 April, a warm spring day. The train grew more crowded as we approached Sheffield's Midland station, towards lunchtime: as usual on a Saturday there was a football match due to take place, at Hillsborough stadium. This weekend was the FA cup semi-final between Liverpool and Nottingham Forest. Jubilant fans, many wearing Liverpool shirts, thronged the carriages.

Late that afternoon, I was having a tranquil cup of tea in the front room of my sister's house when a local radio station broadcast the news of what had happened around 3 p.m., just after kick-off at Hillsborough. There had been a crush on the dangerously overcrowded terraces accessed via the congested Leppings Lane entrance to the stadium, with many injured and dead, including, I would later presume, some of the young fans who had been on the train with me several hours before. The disaster would lead to the deaths of ninety-seven people, the worst catastrophe in British sporting history. The dead, dying and injured were laid out on the pitch. The immediate response from police and ambulance services at the scene was woeful enough, but worse was to come. Just as with the Battle of Orgreave during the miners' strike five years before, the accusations of a cover-up by South Yorkshire police became augmented over the next decades, particularly through evidence heard in April 2016 during the second coroner's inquest into the Hillsborough tragedy.

Previously censored documents submitted to that inquest revealed that senior officers from South Yorkshire police, who had given fake news stories to the press implying that drunkenness and hooliganism on the part of Liverpool fans led to the crush at Hillsborough, rather than the decision-making and delay of the emergency services, were also implicated at Orgreave. The first coroner's inquest had ruled the deaths at Hillsborough as 'accidental'; the second, which only came about because of lengthy campaigns by survivors and the victims' families, ruled that those who died at Hillsborough were 'unlawfully killed due to grossly negligent failures by police and ambulance services to fulfil their duty of care'. To this date, no one has been prosecuted. In January 2023, almost thirty-four years after the Hillsborough tragedy, the chair of The National Police Chiefs' Council (NPCC) made the following statement and admission: 'Police failures were the main cause of the tragedy and have continued to blight the lives of family members ever since.'

As I walked through Sheffield that summer of 1989, I renewed my affection for specific landmarks, many of which would be demolished or altered beyond recognition over the next decades. The controversial Egg Box extension to the town hall, so swiftly (and fictionally) dispatched by a nuclear blast in *Threads*. The Hole in the Road, near Castle Market, conceived as a subterranean precinct for a futuristic city: essentially an open roundabout, like a giant all-seeing eye, with traffic circling above and a concrete space below, accessed by long, silent escalators and ramps, and linked with underpasses. Each Christmas a tall fir tree, laden with decorations, would somehow be inserted into its middle – how, I never knew. St Mary's Church on Bramall Lane, its black silhouette, like a Victorian widow in mourning crinoline, dominating the 'cutlery area' past Hanover Square in Broomhall. No longer blighted by the belching fuel pollution that famously caused even the sparrows to cough, Sheffield still held residues of its sooty centuries in the black grime embedded in hundreds of walls and buildings such as this one. The eventual cleaning and refurbishment of St Mary's would break its eerie spell and make it unrecognisable to me. A beige cement monstrosity, a giant oculus, and a begrimed church – such were the beloved urban lodestars of my youth.

After a few weeks, Giulia left the factory, fed up with the early starts, general hostility, and the physical work. Although we all talked animatedly about quitting on an almost daily basis, Karen, Helen and I stayed on, an amiable threesome, sticking together, covering for each other, addicted to the somnolent spell the heavy factory light cast over us, and of course, needing the money. We daydreamed and were hungry for what the weekends would bring.

Saturday nights were our salvation. We'd dress up in vintage 1950s frocks and Dr Martens and, after vodka slammers at my mother's house, hit the city centre. On more than one occasion my sister, now a parent with two very small children, would be woken by a forlorn reversed-charges phone call at 3 a.m. Exhausted and uncomplaining, she would drive out, her raincoat flung on over pyjamas, to pick up and deliver home the four, or three, or more often, two of us – me and Karen, who lived in a village outside Sheffield and would usually stay over, the trains having long stopped running.

It was on one of these Saturdays, in early August, that we met Brendan.

That Saturday night, the three of us set out to get tanked before going on to meet my old schoolfriend Fay at The Leadmill. We were sniffy about The Leadmill – we preferred the cheaper, less self-conscious clubs and pubs in town – but duly assembled to pre-drink at a favourite pub on Division Street. There was little discrimination in what we drank – invariably we chose the fastest route to inebriation. 'Three double whiskies, please,' I shouted over the noise at the guy behind the bar, who was about our age. He'd been regarding us with amusement for a while as we cavorted and caroused for each other, the only women on our own in the pub, oblivious to the stares and nudges around us. Brendan was a student, studying at one of Sheffield's two universities. He asked me to meet him later, he got off at midnight.

That night and every night for the next month and a half, Brendan and I met up for sex. I would clock off from the factory at 6 p.m., rush home, eat dinner and then go out to meet Brendan. At first I made some excuse to my mother, but soon said nothing at all. It became a point of exquisite tension between us as I returned, fumbling with my door keys, twelve hours later, just in time to shower and change before catching the bus to work and repeating the whole cycle.

Brendan lived not far away, in a rented bedsit. Each morning, at around 6 a.m., when I let myself out at the beginning of what promised to be another scorching day, I would walk home. The road back, deserted at that hour, curved steeply, thronging with birdsong, the trees arching across from either side to meet in the middle, interlocking as if in an embrace, or a state of grace. It was like walking through a cathedral made of green leaves.

Brendan's digs consisted of a large room, with a high ceiling, vast windows overlooking the road, and a shared bathroom up a half-flight of stairs, part of a huge, shabby, converted Victorian house, in which I never encountered any of the other inhabitants. In that room, over many weeks, I was instructed in the art of giving and – most importantly for me – receiving sexual pleasure. Brendan, unprepossessing in demeanour, was nevertheless certain in his actions. Sex until that summer had never really been about my own satisfaction. With Brendan it was a slow revelation. We rarely left the bed, except to change the cassette in his tape recorder over from Edie Brickell to All About Eve.

Parched from hours spent in the hot, dusty room, we would at intervals slug tepid milk straight from the bottle, the only item Brendan ever seemed to keep in his tiny fridge. The one occasion we went on anything resembling a conventional date, to Pizza Hut, we had oddly little to say to each other, and scrambled through the meal in order to get back to that room, and that bed. We used condoms as contraception, which, ever-mindful of egalitarianism, we took it in turns to purchase. After we'd been careless a couple of times, I visited an emergency clinic and obtained a prescription for the morning-after pill, unable to face the inquisitive doctors' surgery at which I'd been registered since childhood, and the chance of my mother finding out. I felt very adult and in control even as I was continually nauseous for two days and nights. Brendan was solicitous, and practical.

Back in Cardiff in October, I acclimatised to a new timetable and the serious work of being a second-year student. Brendan and I wrote occasionally, but by Christmas our correspondence had fizzled out. The short, intense weeks with him had given me a new appreciation of my body, and a sexual confidence I had only pretended at before, but, as with him, I was still struggling to build an emotional connection with any of my current 'conquests'. That changed at the beginning of the autumn term when I met Nicholas. From that point the trajectory of the next eight years, although I couldn't be aware of it at the time, was decided.

If my life as the 1980s ended had been a silent film, it would be at this juncture that the title cards between each sequence would instruct the audience that there was something unforeseen about to launch itself out of nowhere.

Within weeks of meeting, I had stubbornly set my heart on Nicholas, who did not remotely resemble the tall dark-haired stranger of my hitherto incredibly conventional imagination. When we were first introduced (he was doing the same course as one of my housemates), a line from *Great Expectations* thrust itself uncomfortably into my head, Miss Havisham's invocation to Estella over the lovelorn Pip: 'You can break his heart.' A modern languages student, Nick listened only to classical music, was a member of the university's judo team and encouraged me to read *Candide*. He set up a French film club at which we watched *Diva* and *Betty Blue*; posters of the latter adorned every other student's bedroom wall of that period.

As the weather grew colder, we began to break away from the usual Wednesday afternoon gatherings with friends and instead drift off together, sitting outside the library in Cardiff city centre, picnicking on jars of lumpfish caviar and fresh baguettes, or venturing inside the warmth of the old covered market for Nick's favourite dish – faggots and peas – which I always declined to eat. 'But you're from Sheffield!' he would tease me, feigning incredulity, and I would ask him about his own home city, which I'd never visited. But as the end of term approached, we were still only friends.

Nick organised a Christmas party for the French Society at a club in town, and, sensing things might be about to shift, I bought a vintage green lace mini dress for ten pounds at Cardiff antiques market. Afterwards, drunk and freezing and in a state of high excitement on my part at least, I walked with Nick back to my house, where I turned the three bars of the electric fire on full. We sat up till 4 a.m., telling each other about our uncannily similar childhoods – early parental divorce, ramshackle houses, constant lack of money, but plenty of books and access to culture – while chastely drinking tea. I was studying Virginia Woolf's first novel, *The Voyage Out*; after that night of shared confidences, I underlined the sentence '*Did love begin in that way, with the wish to go on talking?*' three times.

During the Christmas break I thought about Nick, and wondered. It was his birthday on New Year's Eve and I posted a card to his home address, determined that the new year and new decade would resolve whatever it was between us. By February, following a group expedition to the cinema to see Peter Greenaway's *The Cook, the Thief, His Wife and Her Lover*, and my judicious wearing of a close-fitting red pinafore dress, we'd had our first kiss. But by late March, we weren't speaking. Nick was adamant that he didn't want a 'relationship', which up until then had consisted of hours of clandestine kissing followed by awkwardness in front of our friends – all of whom knew what was going on – and a daily seesaw of elation and misery for me. My return home to Sheffield that Easter was made all the more dismal due to the sudden death of a family friend, a close contemporary of my sister and brother-in-law from university who had collapsed and died at the bar of Leicester railway station, shortly after ordering a gin and tonic, at the age of forty-two. He had been in Cardiff a few weeks earlier and had taken me to lunch; he had given me a recording of Maria Callas's arias; I was inconsolable. After the funeral, which took place during the Easter holidays, I concluded that Nick and I were meant to be just friends.

Cue the silent film title cards again.

The afternoon before I was due to travel back to Cardiff, I'd been for coffee and cigarettes with Karen and Helen, happy that our three-way bond had lasted and that we found each other's company as compelling as ever. We'd had a few nights out that holiday and planned more for the oncoming summer. There was a note lying casually next to the phone on my return home. 'Brendan called for you.' The house was busy, there was to be a family dinner that evening; in the morning my eldest brother, who had returned from years in Australia to live in the UK, was driving me back to Wales.

I didn't hesitate. Nick doesn't want you; he as much as said so, I told myself, and besides . . . I had experienced a long drought in the past months, constantly waiting on Nick's varying affections, and my own equally unvarying determination that he was 'the one'. As I turned to go straight back out the door, calling to my mother that I wouldn't forget dinner, I hummed Lloyd Cole and the Commotions' 'Cut Me Down'.

Brendan was at home, in the bedsit. I pushed the doorbell triumphantly and within a few minutes, as if the last seven months hadn't happened, we were in bed. His old black-and-white television was on, and the Bette Davis film *Now, Voyager* was playing on BBC2. 'Why wish for the moon, when we have the stars?' Davis reassures her married lover, Paul Henreid. 'Did you know that the book of this film was written by Olive Higgins Prouty, who was Sylvia Plath's sponsor through college?' I asked Brendan rhetorically, during a brief pause in our reunion. 'Who's Sylvia Plath?' he answered.

My mother and soon-to-be stepfather were going to New Zealand until September, when they would return to marry in Sheffield. I would not see them for several months, and yet, after dinner and the family farewells, I went back to the bedsit later that evening – of course I did. Brendan gave me some Pro-Plus and we stayed awake through the night, wired with caffeine tablets, laughing and fucking. Leaving him asleep as it was beginning to grow light, I fancied there was something off, something askew about the cloudy spring air, but I dismissed it. I would never see or hear from him again.

Summer term at Cardiff was heavy with the anxiety of imminent Part One exams. It was also bittersweet, with a sense of imminent change – the following year would be different, with all the language students away on their Erasmus year in Europe while the rest of us would be grimly studying for finals. Nick was due to go to Germany for his year abroad. I worried we would lose touch, as I planned to leave Cardiff for London once I had graduated. I didn't hurry to see him when my brother dropped me off. It was mine and my housemate Alys's birthday the following weekend and we had a big party planned – I expected him to come by.

The party the next Friday didn't turn out exactly as expected. Alys's boyfriend was DJ-ing at the frantically popular indie music night at the Student Union – a regular of ours as a warm-up to the weekend. Our house was in the street next to the Union. The boyfriend, high on being the centre of attention, announced from the DJ booth during the final track (The Jesus and Mary Chain's 'April Skies', in honour of our joint birthday) that there was an after party, everyone was invited, and helpfully gave out our address over the loudspeakers. As a result, the house was overrun with strangers, one of whom thoughtfully added a tab of acid to the carefully concocted bowl of punch. The pre-curated music selection was reduced to two cassettes: Prince's *Lovesexy* and the Stone Roses' eponymous debut album, which played on a loop all night, as the soundtrack to events, which were growing ever more lurid and out of hand. I came across Nick trying to stop a guy I had never seen before from pissing in the hall. He and I seemed strangely sober in a drunk and drugged-up crowd. I suggested we go upstairs – my room was at the top of the house, in the attic. When we got there a large man was heavily asleep on my bed, snoring loudly. No point in trying to wake him up, so we retreated to the middle staircase where we spent the remainder of the party observing the chaos around us. Did we become a couple at that moment? I don't know, but whatever had been problematic between us the preceding term had eased. It was no longer referred to and we began to enjoy spending time with one other again. Though there was still no sex, we would spend nights sleeping in my single bed in the attic, fitting ourselves around the rusty iron spike which protruded from the mattress. I had never thought to ask for the mattress to be exchanged for a better one, I simply accommodated myself around it.

Term wore on. May was as fresh and green and beautiful as a Philip Larkin poem; I knew I was in love with Nick, and while Part Ones drove fear into me, I was confident I'd get through them. I was more tired than usual, but put that down to my unhealthy lifestyle. My period was a bit late, but again that wasn't uncommon. One Saturday morning, fooling around in my friend Rosa's room, I impulsively turned a backward somersault on her bed. Something flipped inside my stomach, or lower, a sensation I'd never felt before. 'Are you OK?' Rosa asked. 'You've gone really pale.'

My breasts felt unbearably sore – surely a sign that my period would come soon? I examined them in front of my convex bedroom mirror, which I'd bought at a junk shop as an approximation of that just glimpsed in Jan van Eyck's 'The Arnolfini Portrait'. The effect of the mirror was to make my reflection as imbalanced as those apprehended in the hall of mirrors at a funfair, but even through the glass's distortion I could see that my nipples were bigger and darker than they'd ever been. I had never marked the days of my menstrual cycle in my diary or obsessed too much about a few days' difference in timing each month. But then I started being sick in the mornings – as discreetly as possible, covering it up as a perpetual hangover – although I had stopped drinking alcohol as it tasted awful for some reason. I persuaded myself to make an appointment with my GP, who took a urine sample and told me to call back in a few days. I tried to push my worry – by now exponential – to the back of my mind and concentrate on studying, just as I had as a teenager when unexplained illness had flooded my body.

It was late on a Friday afternoon when, with utter dread, I called the surgery from the payphone nearest the house. In 1990, patient confidentiality wasn't what it is now: the receptionist immediately told me that my test had come back positive. 'Oh,' I said into the receiver. 'I'll make you an appointment with the doctor for Monday,' she said. Her voice was kind.

The GP surgery was a long, long walk from my house. Because I was on permanent medication for my now underactive thyroid auto-immune condition, I had registered as soon as I'd got to Cardiff and chosen one of the very few practices which offered a female GP service, and which also happened to be furthest away from the main university area.

When I saw her, my GP, heavily and happily pregnant (an irony which has never escaped me), was firm, reasoned and non-judgemental. 'You have three options. You can have the baby and keep it, you can have a termination, or you can have the baby and give it up for adoption. It's your choice, but you are very young and you have your life ahead of you and so I would advise . . .'

I asked for time to think.

'But not for too long. From what you've told me you're seven weeks. If you have a termination after twelve weeks it will be induced labour, much harder to recover from psychologically.'

On autopilot, I bought a crate of riotously expensive peaches from a fruit stall – my contribution to the house dinner that evening – and dragged myself back home. I left the peaches in the kitchen, revolted by their smell, and with it all the heady promise of a summer now ruined, and sat at the foot of the attic stairs, crying. I thought I was alone in the house, but Rosa, who at the beginning of the academic year had drawn the lot for the biggest room, complete with enviable double bed, was working at her desk. She came out when she heard me sobbing. 'What's up?'

I told her. 'The baby isn't Nick's,' I said. 'We haven't . . . yet.'

Rosa sighed heavily. 'What are you going to do?'

'I've no idea.'

She regarded me with her big, thoughtful eyes, and squeezed my hand. 'It'll be OK, I promise.'

For two weeks, over a series of increasingly fraught conversations with family and friends via either the payphone at the theatre bar where I had a part-time job, or in a series of dirty and depressing public telephone boxes, I was urged to have an abortion. I had thought, carelessly, that I would switch to a law degree, have the baby and support it myself. But my arguments fell flat: either reasoned out verbally by others, or inside my own jangled head. I had always been pro-choice in terms of pregnancy, while arrogantly or naively thinking that choice would never apply to me. In all this time I never once thought of Brendan, or of contacting him. What was growing inside me, developing every minute of every day, was mine. I felt both protective of it and terrified of it.

Exams began. Somehow I managed to get though my Part Ones, while rushing out at intervals to throw up. I spent a humiliating half-hour with my (male) personal tutor, who looked hideously embarrassed throughout, after which I had to write a letter to a committee of other lecturers asking permission for the submission of my dissertation on the early novels of Virginia Woolf to be postponed until October. My housemates all knew of my predicament. I still had not told Nick.

Summer was now thickly upon us; the FIFA World Cup had begun in Italy. 'Nessun Dorma' ('None Shall Sleep'), an aria from Puccini's opera *Turandot*, and sung by the tenor Luciano Pavarotti as the theme tune for the World Cup coverage, filled the airwaves. There were football-watching parties at friends' houses accompanied by jugs of Sangria and bottles of beer. I attended none of these. 'None Shall Sleep' seemed an appropriate motif for those hot nights, as, restless and wide awake, I read Margaret Drabble's 1965 novel *The Millstone*, about a young academic who gets pregnant as a result of her first, unremarkable sexual encounter. Drabble's character, Rosamund, decides, controversially for the time, to keep the baby and raise it herself. Is that what *I* should do? Literature had always helped me before, why not now? Panic mounted in waves. The weeks were ticking by; it was June.

One Sunday evening, Nick and I went for a walk in Bute Park, in the grounds of Cardiff Castle. In the dark of the trees, he pressed against me, our hands inside each other's clothes. Whatever I'd wanted to happen for so many months would happen now, I thought, but it was wrong, already my stomach was starting to swell, and I pushed him away. Nick started talking about his impending move to Germany and what that meant for us, and how he really couldn't have a committed relationship for a long time and—

'It doesn't matter now,' I interrupted him, in a voice I didn't recognise as my own – flat, and lifeless. 'I'm pregnant, and I don't know what to do.'

Nick appeared stunned. 'It's got nothing to do with you and me,' I went on. 'It was at Easter, he isn't important, it was a mistake—'

'I should have told you I loved you at Easter,' Nick said, out of nowhere, because by now it was completely dark under the trees. 'Then we'd have been together.'

In *The Voyage Out*, the book's main characters, Terence and Rachel, come to a painful admission in the middle of a South American jungle: '*We love each other,*' *Terence repeated, searching into her face. Their faces were both very pale and quiet, and they said nothing. He was afraid to kiss her again. By degrees she drew close to him, and rested against him. In this position they sat for some time. She said 'Terence' once; he answered 'Rachel'.* That night Nick and I made love properly for the first time, delicately, tenderly, and with an enormous sense of relief.

A couple of days later I endured the familiar bus journey to Cambridge, this time to stay with my brother and his family. The moment to make a decision had come. I was worn out with procrastinating. That night in the park Nick had told me, 'Whatever you decide, I'm here,' but I couldn't put that burden on him. As the bus trundled back into Cardiff he was waiting for me, a forerunner of the years to come, when he and I would travel long distances across Europe to meet each other.

On the morning of 9 July, I entered a general women's hospital on the outskirts of Cardiff. I was to be there for three long days. I forget its name and precise location and have been unable to find it in searches on the internet. Deliberate amnesia undoubtedly has something to do with this. In the few memories I am able to summon up it is a low-level building of red brick, with tall, stiff, angry lupins standing to attention in well-ordered flowerbeds. No question of anything out of control here.

Later that afternoon I saw, for the first and last time, the foetus bouncing along in its own amniotic fluid. I forced myself to look at the ultrasound, at the embryo's carefree perfection, just as I forced myself not to cry at the harsh coldness of the metal speculum inserted inside me the following day and the addition of the pessary which began 'the process'. The girl in the bed next to me on the ward, who was a similar age, was training to be a trapeze artist and about to travel around Europe; like me, a baby was not part of her immediate life plan. We talked in whispers, because the woman in the bed opposite was desperately trying not to miscarry her second pregnancy. There was no division or any privacy here: whatever the stage or aspect of pregnancy, we were all thrown in together.

Coming round after the operation, woozy, queasy from the general anaesthetic and with a dull, heavy ache in my stomach and a giant sanitary towel taped between my legs, I heard the far-off sound of a baby crying, as if from a distant room. But there was no baby in the vicinity. I was ravenous. A still, hot, midsummer day. I could see a small square of navy-blue sky through the barred window across from me. A nurse brought a cup of tea and a corned-beef sandwich. I felt exultant, probably because the pregnancy hormones were still flooding through my body. It was not to last. By contrast the trapeze artist, who beforehand had seemed so matter-of-fact about her own procedure, was curled up on her bed, crying quietly. We would not speak again beyond an awkward goodbye and good luck when it was time to leave the hospital and disappear into our briefly yet momentously interrupted lives.

When I was eventually allowed to take a shower, I noticed a small pool of fresh blood on the floor as I entered the cubicle. I stepped over it; it wasn't mine. Seeing my own blood trickling down the inside of my thighs after months of its absence was a shock: that, and the quantity. Years afterwards, when I experienced a partial miscarriage seven weeks into a longed-for pregnancy, and watched in desperation as a pale grey membrane, like a sheet of slubbed silk, slid out of me into the toilet bowl, I thought of that blood and wondered whose it had been.

On being discharged from the hospital, I asked if 'it' had been a boy or a girl. 'We don't keep the products for histology,' the male doctor snapped, and added, with some exasperation, 'Now, will you be a sensible girl, and go on the pill?' He informed me that I would be due a 'post-natal' check with my GP in six to eight weeks, a fact which seemed distressing, as nothing had been born. I was collected and driven away from Cardiff, and the wrecked summer. Nick sat in the front and I in the back, clinging tightly to his hand, before he was dropped off to catch the bus back to his own city. Two days later, as I recuperated in Cambridge, someone asked why I was crying.

I took my five-year-old niece to the botanical gardens, making sure her halo of dark curls was fully in my range of sight as she skipped around the lily pond. The petals of the lily pads seemed to plead with me like the outstretched hands of a child I would never know.

My niece ran towards me, arms wide, wanting to be lifted up in my arms, her mouth opened in a smile to reveal a row of perfect white milk teeth.

Chapter Eight

Shiny Happy People

There was something wrong with the house. It had a blank, shuttered look, as if the windows, should you attempt to glimpse yourself in the glass, would reflect nothing back but their own vacancy. Inside, despite the fresh white paintwork and new apple-green carpets, the large rooms and high ceilings, the impression was one not of space, but of a watchful claustrophobia. The long narrow hallway was dark, vehemently closed off from sunlight, the only indication of the street outside the oddly muffled noise of traffic. The landlord had a false bonhomie which I mistrusted instantly. Yet there were practical advantages to the place that we couldn't overlook. On paper, this was going to be much the best house we had inhabited in our three years in Cardiff, having endured mouldy bathrooms, damp bedrooms, mice and worse. It even possessed a washing machine and tumble-dryer – no more interminable Sunday afternoons in the launderette – and central heating, a thrill after autumns and winters wrapped in sour sweat-soaked woollen layers which never warmed us, with only the fierce, headache-inducing blast of an electric fire to take off some of the chill. Location-wise, it was perfect: round the corner from Albany Road, in the heart of student Cardiff.

The times were changing, one year into the 1990s: Eastern Europe was coming in from the cold and the local deli made and sold its own pesto. Even so, the Edwardian era, of which the house was firmly a part, permeated everywhere. Just up the road from the house was Roath Park, with its swans, whistling ducks, ornamental lake and lighthouse memorial to Captain Scott's doomed Antarctic expedition – the *Terra Nova* having sailed from Cardiff on 15 June 1910.

Three of us, newly graduated with shiny degrees, had been tasked to find a house for five – two more would be returning imminently from Spain and from Italy. For the first time in over a year our contingent – Alys, Rosa, Delyth, Meinir, and me – would all be living together again, unmet since the previous New Year's Eve, when we had gathered, raucously, a few streets away, to celebrate the twenty-first birthday of Nick, now my boyfriend.

It was late August when we moved into the house. The weather was hot, as ominously unbroken as Bryan Adams's reign at the number one spot in the charts with 'Everything I Do' – the unceasingly popular theme tune from the film *Robin Hood, Prince of Thieves*. It would tyrannise the airwaves for sixteen weeks, July to November, an expanse of time which would take us from the revels and solemnity of graduation, to a birthday sodden with tears because one of us would never again mark another year. We mocked it, of course, because we were cool indie kids. And yet its lyrics somehow insinuated themselves like a splinter under a fingernail.

When we moved into our new place on that hot August afternoon, I had not yet read Elizabeth Bowen's supernatural wartime story 'The Demon Lover', but coming across it in a London library a year later it seemed to exactly describe the slow malignancy of the house in Cardiff. *Dead air came out to meet her as she went in.*

I omitted to mention my reservations to the others, and once Rosa arrived back, happy and tanned from her half-year abroad in Spain, we duly drew lots for the bedrooms. Mine was a smallish room which overlooked the back garden – hardly a garden, more an excess of earth and rubble. Our landlord's real estate primping didn't extend to the externals – we were only students, after all, just there to pay him a year's rent before the next intake arrived. Rosa had drawn the large, spacious ground-floor front room with the bay window, but she was reluctant, having already enjoyed the best room in our previous second-year house. 'I think Alys should have it' – the fifth member of the household, who was due back in a couple of weeks. Instead, Rosa insisted on a tiny room upstairs, next to my own, which contained a rather childlike bunk bed. I thought it was brave of her to sleep on the top bunk, but then it was me who feared any kind of height, not Rosa.

I had bought an emerald bar of apple-scented soap from The Body Shop and left it in the bathroom for general use. It became a daily in-joke. The soap! The fragrance! The colour so beautifully matching the green of the carpets! The sharp-sweet aroma of apples unbearable since then. Season of mists and mellow fruitlessness.

In Cardiff, even at this end point of summer, it was green, green everywhere. The dusty, dark green of Ilex leaves and drooping trees. On the radio, The Shamen sang of being able to move any mountain, and at that point in our lives it is possible we felt some aspect of this confidence, but my main memory is of being listless and jangly, and I blamed the house.

Nick was away in south-west France for the remainder of the summer, working on a farm. Having spent his entire year abroad in Germany he now needed to show evidence of immersion in the French part of his degree, and so he went to Marmande, where the sweetness of the tomatoes he was picking tasted like nothing else, or so he told me. He would be back later in September. In the meantime, we wrote of our desire for each other, every few days, frustratedly, and crossly. My low-level anxiety seeped into the pages.

Soon after we moved into the new house, it was Meinir's twenty-first birthday, falling on the bank holiday week-end. People thronged to the house. Although Nick wasn't there, his brother and a couple of his friends stayed; others, belatedly accommodation-hunting for the next college year, camped out in our living room or in the still-empty bedrooms. We boozed, we ate, we lazed and talked, we lamented the continuing musical dominance of Bryan Adams, we danced. Awake until dawn, the psychedelic, sashaying chords of Primal Scream's recently released 'Higher Than the Sun' trembled and shimmered in the haze of a long-drawn-out summer, a last burst of student life before the seriousness of proper adulthood took hold. Rosa and me, manic with exuberance and drink, laughing so much it hurt, held on to each other throughout REM's 'Shiny Happy People', shouting the words in each other's faces.

One morning that weekend, after a particularly late night, stumbling from my bedroom to the bathroom, I noticed that Rosa had fallen asleep in the box room, the door flagrantly wide open to the corridor. All I could see of her were her legs and feet sticking out from under a duvet. *Like a corpse*, I thought momentarily, and then just as quickly forgot the thought.

The house, meanwhile, watched, and waited. The long days of partying ended, our guests left, we cleared up the mess, took out the bottles and settled down to await the autumn.

In the weeks before Alys's return Rosa drifted between both of their rooms, using the larger downstairs one to give English lessons at what I considered to be an exorbitant rate; she'd been teaching in Spain. 'I have an overdraft,' she shrugged, when I exclaimed. My own overdraft was also in contention, as long letters to and from the bank testified, an epistolary relationship I did not welcome. Having graduated, I had finished one official – and funded – part of my life and it would be a while before I embarked on the next, so to pay rent I had to get a part-time job.

Jobs in the city were scarce. Cardiff at this period was in the throes of transformation and its unwanted, unshakeable twin, apprehension. When I'd arrived at the end of the 1980s the university itself was on the brink of insolvency, averted by a merger with the University of Wales Institute of Science and Technology. The city's redevelopment was, at this point, very much in its infancy. The Cardiff I knew was a place of Victorian and Edwardian shopping arcades, the imposing and historic Howells and David Morgan department stores, the less imposing C&A and Littlewoods (where on Fridays we would stock up with cheap bottles of gin for the weekend), the central indoor market (once the site of a gallows) with its giant H. Samuel clock at the entrance – with little in the way then of swanky hotels or high rises.

Just beyond the market, Butetown, where the docks were, was generally no-go, but the previous summer, Delyth and I had attended a wondrous production there one hot, dry afternoon. In the Grade II-listed St Stephen's Church, *A Midsummer Night's Dream* was staged by Moving Being Theatre. The church's formal interior surrendered itself to a spellbinding sylvan scene in which the actors, moving among dark green cardboard trees and wearing bright paper horses' heads, seduced us with transformation, slinking among a charmed audience to offer a picnic of apples and honey cakes. A strangely otherworldly production in a place that was rumbling with bulldozers, scaffolding, and regeneration.

Later that same year, on a black November evening, I was in Butetown again, earning money as an extra in a Reclaim the Night march, a scene in a film I never knew the name of. The extras were paid fifteen pounds each and the scene was later cut. I felt uneasy during the shoot, not least because of the film's topic. The winter before I arrived in Cardiff, a brutal murder took place in Butetown; still unsolved that November, it cast a pall over the whole city. On the evening of Valentine's Day 1988, twenty-year-old Lynette White, who had worked as a prostitute in the area, was found dead in a grim first-floor flat above a betting shop in James Street. Her substantial and dire injuries included a viciously cut throat and a body that had been stabbed so many times her T-shirt resembled a bloody doily.

How had I still not clearly recognised that violence against women was endemic and ongoing, despite growing up under the swarming, furious cloud of the man known as the Yorkshire Ripper? Perhaps I had simply been reassured so many times and so had come to believe that dreadful incidents, especially killings by strangers, were isolated.

As ever, the onus on women and girls was to stay alert at all times. At school we had been instructed not to 'give men the wrong idea', a hopeless diktat straight out of its Victorian playbook. In these years at university I experienced my own share of what I now realise were assaults – covert and unsolicited pawing of my breasts, or between my legs. There was also the ever-present danger of unexpected mob attack, disguised as 'banter'. One Sunday evening during our second year, when a friend and I were having a quiet drink in the deserted Tafarn, the usually crowded Student Union pub, a group of male students fresh from rugby practice came in. We were the only women in 'their' space, and they surrounded us, pulling at our hair. When one squeezed my friend's breast so that she cried out in pain and fear, I stepped in to defend her, only to have a full ice bucket tipped over my head. The man working alone behind the bar did nothing, probably as frightened as we were. We fled and avoided the bar on Sunday evenings ever after. We also never reported it. Who would we tell?

Despite this omnipresent harassment, for the most part our group of friends was irrepressible, robust, gobby, curious and – generally – happy. Photographs taken over the three years brim with deliriousness, defiance, humour and love. There was a dark magic to being young, to being free. On Monday mornings in our first year, ahead of the 9 a.m. lecture on twentieth-century poetry, Carys, whose room was next to mine, would sling The Smiths' 'Unhappy Birthday' onto her portable turntable; at the same moment I would, in answer, press my tape player button on The Jesus and Mary Chain's 'Darklands', before, arm in arm, we hurried off though the shrouding autumn mist, breakfastless, weary and completely alive. Nihilism seemed a beautiful plaything at that age.

But now, three years later, I was beginning to face up to the realities of life as an adult. I applied for a job at the main bookshop in the city centre. After an interview, I was hired to work three days a week in the travel section. I tried to hide my disappointment – I wanted to show off my new degree by selling (and reading) fiction. The role was initially to be shared with an unsmiling young woman of about my own age who had worked at the bookshop before. Once both of our probationary periods were up, one of us would be made permanent. At the time I didn't quite grasp the awkwardness of this plan or the evident resentment of my new colleague.

August became September with unseemly suddenness. On Monday 2nd I wasn't working, and I went with Rosa into town. She wanted to buy new clothes. Oasis had recently opened as a chain of stores, and its shop on Queen Street boasted a sleek, minimalist interior, more like a boutique than a chain. Rosa flicked through the rails and tried things on, buying a surprising amount of stuff. 'I thought you said you had an overdraft?' She laughed. 'I do . . . but I don't care.' I admired her in a bright green halter-neck top, the colour of the apple soap and the wretched carpets, for which I was beginning to experience an inexplicable aversion, but it looked beautiful on her.

Rosa had changed over the last year away from our clique, lost some of her shyness, her reticence, her holding back. There was a gleam to our friends who had been away in Europe having adventures, while we, the left behind, drably slogged over our finals. Sometimes characteristics of this new confidence were expressed abruptly, jarringly. Anecdotes about people and places we had never encountered, experiences we couldn't have, occasionally came out as arrogant and boastful. We were envious, too, of the year of university they still had ahead of them, without responsibility or the dull jobs we found ourselves in. It would take time to adjust. But we had time.

Tuesday 3 September. Still hot, and I was at work in the bookshop all day, trying to get to grips with the cash register, the credit-card machine and the increasingly hostile presence of my co-worker. That evening, the conversation in the house between the five of us there – our friend Angharad was staying temporarily while looking for a house-share – turned darkly morbid. We discussed at some length which we would prefer: burial, or cremation? I usually shrank from such debates, wary of dwelling on the not-being. Rosa was emphatic. 'I want to be cremated. I don't want to be put in a box in the ground.' I don't recall what the rest of us said. We wrapped up, went off to bed.

Next morning, Wednesday 4 September, Rosa got up around the same time as me: she had someone arriving for an early English lesson. I showed her a recent photograph of Nick, whom she hadn't seen for nine months: 'He looks like an angel!' He did. I decided I would buy a phone card at lunchtime and call Nick in France that evening. The house didn't yet have a telephone connected but there was a phone box just down the street.

Delyth met me after work; a regular informal arrangement, as her job was twenty minutes away from Cardiff; she commuted by train and passed the bookshop each day on her walk from the station. Neither of us had settled into our immediate post-graduation life; we were tired, dissatisfied. Walking slowly back home that evening, our discussion kept circling back to the 'new' Rosa, whose fresh confidence and resulting independence from us was causing tension.

Phone call to Nick made, I was chopping mushrooms for a risotto when Rosa came downstairs and into the kitchen. 'Are you having supper?' I asked. She was dressed to go out: wide-legged black trousers (they would later be referred to as 'slacks'), a brown scoop-necked top decorated with large purple and blue flowers, the same worn-in Dr Martens we all wore, a brown leather bag with the strap across her body. I could smell her perfume, Dior's Poison, heavy and sickly, like flowers at the moment of decay. *Poison isn't a fragrance you wear, it's a fragrance that wears you.* 'I'm going to meet a friend in the Four Bars,' she replied, somewhat evasively, without acknowledging that we both knew who the friend was – the guy she'd invited to the party over the weekend, the one she'd used to know back at home.

There was a pause, then Meinir came in. 'I'm going out too, I'll walk with you into town.' Chatting, they strode down the long corridor, shouting back goodbyes as they went. A bright burst of evening sunshine as the door opened, then the hall was slammed into darkness again. I carried on slicing mushrooms, and Delyth and I cooked and ate in silence.

The weather broke next morning, in the early hours of Thursday 5 September. I opened my bedroom curtains in time to witness a cat taking a leisurely shit among the debris of the back garden, a miserable scene wreathed in mist and drizzle. Setting the mood for today, I thought, as the cat's eyes and mine briefly locked in a fizz of mutual hostility, before I went next door to Rosa's room to borrow a belt. I was wearing what passed for 'smart' clothes for work – a pair of slim linen shorts, olive green with white spots, a white T-shirt and an oversized green cardigan. My too-long hair was tied back with a green velvet scrunchie. What was it with green and this house? We all seemed to be infected with the colour.

Expecting a bleary, hungover Rosa to be yawning on the top bunk, I was surprised to find that her room was empty. I had never known her not to come home at night before, but there was always a first time. Picking up the belt, threading it through the loops of my shorts, I noticed rain spattering through the open window onto Rosa's desk propped up against the sill. Leaning forward, I slammed the window shut so hard that it jumped and rattled in its frame. Stepping over Rosa's towel on the floor, still damp from her shower the previous evening, I almost tripped over her splayed, plugged-in hairdryer. I was in a hurry; it was already 8:30 a.m. I was due at the bookshop for 9 and invariably arrived a few minutes after. There was none of the indulgence I'd been shown as a student when, in my second year, my tutor had moved the hour of our Friday morning meeting from 10 to 11 a.m. because, as I earnestly explained, I *had* to attend HMV Dance Night at the Student Union the night before.

It was one minute after nine as I slipped in, the daily meeting with all staff attending already begun. The morning passed in a blur, my silent antagonist of a co-worker beside me. Taking a phone call from a customer, I was pleased to resolve a query myself without consulting anyone else. At lunchtime I sat – alone as usual – in the dingy staffroom, eating my sandwich and drinking through a straw from my miniature carton of Just Juice, acutely aware of the loud slurping noise it made. I longed for Nick, his physical proximity, even though the summer had been filled with rows and reconciliations. I wondered without interest whether Bryan Adams would still be at number one on *Top of the Pops* that evening. Probably.

Relief as 5 p.m. came around. Surreptitious glancing at the travel section's clock all day – I never wore a watch. The rain had cleared: through the main entrance to the bookshop drifted blazing swatches of early evening sun. Up a side passage, serving as a short cut to Queen Street, Delyth was leaning against the wall ahead of me. Pleased, although we hadn't planned to meet, I moved towards her, smiling. But Delyth's face was pale, and she was shrinking into the wall, as if trying to hide from an onslaught visible only to her.

'*I don't know how to tell you this,*' slowly, dazed, licking her lips, which were dry and as grey as the rest of her skin, '*but Rosa has been found dead in a house in —— Road.*'

Did someone kill her.

Did someone give her drugs.

(None of us took drugs, we 'just' drank too much alcohol.)

I don't know.

Delyth's older sister and a friend were waiting for us in a car in Park Place, to drive us home. Meinir was there; the police had visited her at lunchtime, verifying identification, tipped off by someone in that house in —— Road, who remembered the unusual first name of one of Rosa's friends.

The house in which Rosa had died was in Pontcanna, a suburb to the west – huge Victorian villas; a long, long street lined with trees. Decades later I would recognise it in the BBC television adaptation of Philip Pullman's *His Dark Materials*, standing in for a similar area of Oxford, as the time travellers move back and forth between worlds. Watching one episode, I had an urge to reach into the portal and snatch Rosa back from that terrible day in 1991, return her to the life she left, to all the life she missed out on.

We stumbled along Queen Street, gasping, sobbing, trying to hold each other up. In the car, Delyth's sister and her friend were silent and grim-faced in the front. We got in the back, holding hands.

The house retained its sinister blank look, of course it did.

The front door open, the hated hallway full of people. As I went in with Delyth, they grabbed at us, faces full of commiseration and sympathy. Meinir was sitting on the sofa in the living room at the back of the house, staring at nothing. We flung ourselves at her. 'The police came,' she told us, in a monotone. 'They asked, do you know Rosa ——?' When I told them yes, they said:

'*We are very sorry to have to tell you that she has passed away.*'

Tears trickled down Meinir's face. Someone placed a mug of hot, sweet tea in my hand. I didn't take sugar in tea or coffee but I drank it down, anything to control the shaking from head to foot that had overtaken my body.

Passed away.

Passed into nothingness.

I came to with a jolt. Her family. We must—

'They know,' Meinir said, tonelessly. 'The local police.' I had an image of a nervous young constable knocking on the door of Rosa's family home about to deliver the worst news of their lives.

Someone was pushing through the mass of people. It was Angharad. 'What's happened?' Delyth hesitated, cleared her throat, then we all spoke at once; Angharad's face crumbled. Angharad had grown up with Rosa, had known her since childhood. The same sentences had to be said over and over, and still we couldn't believe them.

So what did happen?

At 8:30 that morning, at the same moment I was closing Rosa's bedroom window against the sudden squall of rain, a person leaving their ground-floor flat in —— Road came across the body of a young woman in the passageway at the side of the house. Lying on her back, eyes open, fully dressed apart from her feet, which were bare. High above her, so many storeys above, the wide, gaping window of the room from which she had somehow descended.

The usual occupant of that room, situated in a flat on the very top floor of the house, was still asleep on the bed directly adjacent to the open window when the police arrived.

So what did happen?

The police quickly established that the occupant of that room, the person with Rosa that night, had nothing to do with her death.

So what did happen?

That evening we traipsed to and from the phone box down the street or up the street, or to our next-door neighbours, who had a telephone and let us use it to contact our families. After I'd spoken to mine, I called Nick in France. He came on the line, impatient, what was it, we'd only talked the night before, he was in the middle of dinner. '*I don't know how to tell you this,*' I began. He said nothing and I repeated myself, thinking he hadn't heard me, but the silence that met me was his shock. 'Come back,' I said. 'I need you.'

Then we were alone. Night spooled around us. Just the four of us, in this house meant for five. We slept – if we slept at all – huddled on the sofa and chairs in the living room, too afraid to separate. Going up in pairs to the next floor, to gather duvets and pillows or to use the bathroom, thankfully at the other end of the corridor from Rosa's room. When I entered my own room to collect a few items, the light from the street lamp outside her window, curtains unclosed, filtered out into the hallway. There was no visible moon. It was in its last, waning quarter. In a few days a new moon would rise. I couldn't bear the room's achingly open door and made a sudden rush at it, forcing it shut, closing off her room, entombing everything in there. It would be several days before any of us saw inside again, as the bedroom doors automatically locked when shut, only accessed by their key holders. The following week, our landlord released the door; at the same time, he demanded that we cover Rosa's unpaid rent. Her first month's cheque had been returned from the bank, with 'Deceased' scrawled over it.

Friday at first light, stiff, sore, and cold, we witnessed the morning arrive, the sky owlish grey smeared with rusty red, like old blood.

A trudge to the phone box again, to call our places of work and tell them we wouldn't be coming in. 'Take all the time you need,' said my manager; the news had been on local radio. Reporters flapped at our letter box throughout the day; we refused to engage. Friends turned up, stupefied and weeping; many we had seen the previous weekend, for Meinir's birthday party. A couple of police officers – gentle, and careful, came to ask questions: about Rosa's mood over the last few days, her habits, anything that might give a reason for her to . . . 'She used to sleepwalk,'

Delyth told them, and so she did. More than once, in our second year, Rosa left our house in the middle of the night in pyjamas and we had to chase after her down the street. Glassy-eyed, docile, she allowed us to lead her back to bed and tuck her in, regarding us with astonishment the next morning when we recounted her nocturnal activities, of which she remembered nothing. 'And she had a bunk bed here,' I said. They asked to see it, but of course I had locked the door.

That evening we had to get a doctor, as someone was having a panic attack. The doctor advised us not to stay in the house. But where could we go? We were waiting for Rosa to come back. Earlier that week, Meinir had cut out strips of paper, written our names on them, and stuck them above the coat hooks next to the front door. Rosa's was the last. 'Peg R' it proclaimed, but the coat hook was empty. At some point Meinir removed the pieces of paper. When someone new moved into Rosa's room a few weeks later, we didn't replace the names.

Saturday, late morning, I was still in my dressing gown, hair tangled, when the doorbell rang. On the front step, Alys, who was still due to move in, and had flown back early from Europe. Stricken. This house was supposed to be the scene of a reunion, instead it had become the site of a wake. Over tears and tea in chipped mugs, Alys said: '*Tell me what happened.*'

'*It was a very warm night.*'

'*Stop, go back, start again, before that . . .*'

The night before Rosa's funeral, seven of us gathered at a house on the coast, lent for the purpose by someone's family. Nick had not yet returned from France. We cooked, talked, played music, cautiously drank a little wine. Before bed, we walked on the shingled beach. Waves crashed, abundantly, as they always did and always would. Without speaking, Delyth pressed some shells she had collected into each of our hands. I still have mine, although it, like my memories of that time, keeps breaking up into smaller and smaller pieces. It lies in a small round wooden box with a green lid on which is painted a wobbly black-and-white cat, along with the gold-and-brown striped tiger's eye Nick bought me in Amsterdam, and the giant silver daisy symbol I wore on a cord around my neck throughout all the summers of love.

Relics.

That afternoon, we had driven over to Rosa's home, The La's playing on the car radio, a collective sob when 'There She Goes' came on. We had not yet seen any of Rosa's family apart from one relative, who had arrived in Cardiff a few days before to collect Rosa's belongings. The door to Rosa's room now unlocked, Delyth and I had performed the task of sorting and packing, shunting clothes and books, folders, tapes, CDs, jewellery and cosmetics, ornaments, paper, pens, bedding, the contents of the waste basket, into Rosa's suitcases or into black bin liners. We did not exchange a word during this process. When the door was opened, I half expected everything to be coated in dust – it seemed that centuries had already passed. The green towel remained on the floor just as she had left it, the hairdryer plugged into the wall. Air heavy with the cloying scent of Poison. The extravagant purple bottle, with gold lettering and a giant glass stopper, I laid carefully among her clothes, so that it wouldn't break. I went through Rosa's address book and copied down lists of friends she had made on her year abroad; someone had to write to them. '*You don't know me, but.*' '*I'm so sorry to have to tell you that.*' '*The funeral is taking place on.*' There was a name and address for the house on —— Road, written in Rosa's elegant, upright hand. The last item to be sealed away was the green halter-neck top which Rosa had bought on our shopping excursion three days before she died, and which she never wore.

The visit to Rosa's family was the hardest. Her mother talked rapidly in a low murmur, while Rosa's father sat silently beside her. I tried to avert my eyes from the wreaths in the corner – one composed of the letters of Rosa's name, the other a harp (*telyn*) made of flowers. A younger Rosa had played the harp in competition at the annual Eisteddfod. As her mother passed around recent photographs, Rosa's father started to weep without sound, shoulders shaking. Tears poured into our teacups. None of us could look at each other.

We visited the site of the grave, alone, in the churchyard, which was at the top of a steep incline. The freshly prepared hole in the earth was an obscenity. Someone next to me began to wail. *'I don't want to be put in a box in the ground,'* Rosa had said, only a few days before.

Gathered around the grave the next morning, we each threw in an individual red rose after the coffin had been lowered. The sound of sobbing, mingled with birdsong, seemed to echo to the tops of the purple mountains surrounding the valley, up and up into the huge, endless sky. In a borrowed long black silk skirt, I felt a familiar thud as blood slid into my underwear – my period had come early. Life continuing.

It seemed the entire community had come out for the funeral. As we turned away from the grave, people fell aside to let us pass. Delyth's and Meinir's parents were there among the crowd, hands outstretched to us. At the bottom of the hill, friends were standing, frozen in bewilderment. One figure was alone, clinging to the fence, hair askew, face red and wrung out with crying. The young man with whom Rosa had spent her last evening.

Much later, Delyth and I lay separately awake throughout the night in twin beds at her home in Flintshire. She saw me off from Crewe the following day: I was going to Sheffield for the weekend before returning to Cardiff. As the train pulled out of the station, Delyth raised her arm in what was almost a salute. Her face was set.

Arriving in Sheffield, there was no one to meet me. I took a taxi to my sister's house in Broomhall. As I got out of the cab, the front door opened. My mother, my stepfather close behind her, ran down the steps to gather me in.

Autumn. We remained in the house, for whatever reason. At night, I slept with my bedside lamp on, but it didn't prevent the nightmares. I often dreamt of Rosa. She was with us, walking down the street, trying to attract our attention, but we ignored her. 'She doesn't know she's dead,' I thought. In another dream, I encountered her in a landscape of trees and fields and hills, empty apart from the two of us. 'I'm so bored,' Rosa told me, mournfully, a line that could be straight out of one of our favourite films, *Heathers*.

Once I awoke to see her rummaging through one of the drawers in my room. There was something wrong with the back of her head. What was she looking for? After we packed her possessions away, I realised I still had the belt I'd borrowed the morning she was found, along with a navy-blue cotton jumper she'd lent me the week before. I kept them for years, until they wore out or got lost in one of my many subsequent house moves.

Relics.

Alys moved into her appointed front room, and soon the household was joined by two sweet-natured men: Lewis, an old friend of Rosa's who moved, allegedly undaunted, into the room with the bunk bed, and Alessandru. Alessandru was in Cardiff for a year from Italy to learn English, which, thanks to Alys's tutelage, he spoke with a strong Welsh accent. Nick, now back from France, was renting a room in a house closer to Roath Park, with some postgrads.

We had waited for so long to be in the same place again, and now it was profoundly difficult between us. Everything seemed in flux.

My career at the bookshop ended abruptly at the beginning of October. One Monday morning I was called into the manager's office, to be told that my work wasn't up to scratch, there had been complaints – most, as it turned out, made by my co-worker. 'You can work until the end of this week.' Exiting the office, I went directly to the staffroom and picked up my coat and bag. Disconsolate, I trailed through the town centre, and back to Nick's house, which I had left an hour or so before. I could guarantee he'd still be where I'd left him, asleep in bed. I couldn't go to my own house because everyone would be at work or college and I was too afraid to be there by myself. Nick was not especially pleased to see me but relented when I cried and railed against – well, everything. We stayed in bed all of that day.

How I was I going to pay the rent? It had taken weeks to find this job, how would I get another? I was only seeking short-term temporary work – I was also applying to postgraduate publishing courses far away from Cardiff. My degree overqualified me, and my lack of practical experience underqualified me. In the end, I found shift work at the bar I had worked in during my second and third years, along with Alys and Angharad, and Rosa, and at the Reject Shop in the new Queen Street retail centre. I spent monotonous hours stacking shelves with cheap, badly made objects, and serving behind the till. Red Dragon Radio, the local station, blared incessantly through a speaker above the shop's door. On 5 November, while I was artfully arranging a display of Teenage Mutant Ninja Turtle slippers, the news came in that the newspaper tycoon Robert Maxwell had been found floating dead in the sea after disappearing from his yacht, the *Lady Ghislaine*, moored in the Canary Islands. Does this count as a JFK moment, I wondered, at the precise second a mountain of fluffy Teenage Mutants collapsed on top of me.

The day we'd been dreading arrived: that of Rosa's inquest. Getting dressed that morning, I thought of the freezing night in 1989 we did the Mumbles Mile – the legendary pub crawl along Swansea's seafront, where we'd been visiting friends for the weekend – Rosa, with the midnight sea behind her, swinging a wine bottle and belting out 'New York, New York'. And Valentine's Day 1990, when, drunk, she and Nick and I lurched our way into a performance of *Cosi Fan Tutte* at the New Theatre, narrowly avoiding being ejected for giggling, and, in Rosa's case, falling asleep and snoring, after which Nick fried eggs in our kitchen, and we ate them dancing around Rosa's bedroom while her record player blared out Ella Fitzgerald singing 'My Funny Valentine'.

The coroner was elderly, crisp, assiduous. Delyth, nervous but clear, had to give evidence of Rosa's sleepwalking habits, as she had witnessed the most episodes. We heard for the first time the trajectory of Rosa's final evening – the meeting in the Four Bars, on to a couple of other pubs, the amount of cider drunk, then back to the top-floor flat in —— Road, music played, the crashing out on the bed adjoining the window fatally open to the sultry September night. Then nothing until the next morning at 8:30. Another witness called to give evidence told the court they might have heard a faint noise at around 3 a.m. Perhaps that was when Rosa departed the world. The coroner ruled a verdict of accidental death.

So what did happen?

This is what I believe happened: Rosa, half asleep, tipsy, maybe dreaming, and in an unfamiliar place, must have thought she was in her own bedroom, lying on the top bunk. Swinging her legs over what she supposed was the side of her bed, she sailed out of the window into the black night beyond.

Cameras flashed at us as we left the courthouse; later on the local TV news I spotted the hood of the red duffle coat I was wearing – my *Don't Look Now* coat, as I joked to no one but myself – and Nick walking next to me, his arm around me, pulling me away. Famished, as none of us had had breakfast, we assembled at the Park Vaults pub for pints of creamy Guinness and plates of greasy chips.

Later in November, it was, or would have been, Rosa's twenty-second birthday. To mark it, our friend Hari's Welsh-language grunge band played a gig in celebration of our friend. The evening was cathartic. We had only recently started going out properly again. The first time, dancing to Prince's 'Get Off' in a pair of black micro shorts and a dusty pink ribbed top which Rosa had persuaded me to buy on that September Monday in Oasis, was almost an out-of-body experience: an astonishment that it could still be enjoyable. The gig for Rosa, where we wept and laughed in equal measure, was also the last occasion on which we were all harmoniously together. We were diverging, taking new paths, intent on the future.

On 24 November Freddie Mercury died: a huge shock, as the statement that he had AIDS had only been put out the previous day. Nick and I holed up in his room, playing Queen songs. I thought of my childhood crush on Freddie's long eyelashes; and also the odd coincidence that a cousin of his – a shy, pleasant young man – was our contemporary here at university.

I was still sleeping badly, even when Nick stayed the night with me in my narrow bed. I annoyed him by insisting on keeping the lamp on. But somehow staying at Nick's was even worse. His room, at the very back of a sprawling house, was removed from the other bedrooms and always cold, no matter how much we cranked up the heating. A mouse-grey, ashy pall seemed to hang over it, the bare bulb in the ceiling light never bright enough. I dreamt I was mummified in a winding sheet, or worse, that cold hands were clamped around my neck, in the process of strangling me. Whenever I fought myself awake, Nick was sleeping serenely beside me. I was certain that something had happened in this room, something terrible. I conveyed my fears. Nick looked at me as if I were mad. Perhaps I was.

The year dragged to its close. On its last day, Nick's birthday, there was time to spare after my shift at the Reject Shop, before catching the train to his home town to join him to see in the new year. On impulse I went into Warehouse and tried on a dress; I had some Christmas money to spend. Dark, mossy green, made of slubby velveteen, the dress was very short and very tight with a high neck, puffed-out shirred sleeves and a bodice which resembled an Elizabethan doublet. A Penelope Taberner Cameron for the 1990s, a Greensleeves for the last decade of the twentieth century. My never-forgotten love for the fictional Derbyshire farmhouse Thackers, and the story contained within *A Traveller in Time*, endured. I kept the dress on while I paid and the sales assistant wrapped up my other clothes. Forever green, just as the Pixies sang in 'Velouria'.

Nick met me from the train, our kisses a blazon against the frosty air. I wished him happy birthday. 'Do you like your present?' I asked, slowly unbuttoning my coat, and placing his hands inside. He caressed the velvet.

Crowds gathered in front of the abbey in Nick's town on a starlit midnight as the bells rang in 1992. I swallowed a sob, and he and I decamped to a pub to knock back tequila slammers until daybreak.

To the next year.

To the rest of our lives.

To nothing and to no one, whispered a voice inside my head.

1992, a historic year for Europe. The former Soviet bloc was thawing rapidly, and on 7 February, paving the way for a single European currency, the Maastricht Treaty was signed in the Netherlands, establishing a European Union, free movement between member states, closer collaboration of foreign and security policy, justice and human rights. Ratified by its then twelve members including the United Kingdom, it would rise to twenty-eight members, until the UK's 2016 referendum signalled the ill-thought-out departure known as Brexit.

My few short years at university had witnessed a seesaw of freedoms and oppression. In February 1989, the fatwa was imposed on Salman Rushdie; we happened to be studying his novel *Shame* the week that he was forced to go into hiding. That summer, in June, came the violent crackdown against the student protests in Tiananmen Square, in Beijing, the leftover piles of broken bicycles all that remained of a crushed, fleeting uprising. In November, the Berlin Wall fell.

One chilly Sunday morning in February 1990, our household had risen unusually early, and, wrapped in duvets and with mugs of steaming tea, gathered around the small television set to glimpse the world's most famous political prisoner for the first time in our lives. Incarcerated since 1962, before any of us had been born, and not seen in public since 1964, Nelson Mandela walked free, dignified in a dark grey suit, on a sparkling Cape Town afternoon.

The frosty temperatures of that morning had been warmed by friendship and shared emotions. Two years later, the situation couldn't be more different. Since Rosa's death the walls of the house had been leaning in, eavesdropping, whispering through the cracks now visible underneath the formerly pristine paint. The growing froideur among us was obvious. We were separating, messily. It was not immediately apparent; we were all busy. But our usual mixture of Welsh and English was now, more often than not, simply Welsh – which would be fine if I were anywhere near fluent and understood properly.

As a response I leant more heavily on Nick, so much so that his household must have loathed the sight of me, forlornly appearing at their front door or on the other end of the telephone. But all seemed to be disintegrating with us, too. We were fighting more and more, most often in public. I was anxious and possessive and had a highly developed sense of drama. Once, at a party, following a vicious row, Nick threw a glass of red wine in my face, and I became hysterical. No one was remotely sympathetic.

On the second Sunday in February Nick walked me to Cardiff railway station; the wind was biting, sleet dropping in clumps from a blank sky. I dragged my unwieldy suitcase behind me. Only Meinir accompanied me to the door. The others had not looked up to say goodbye as I left the house. As the train pulled out, Nick and I gazed at each other through the misted glass. His face was white in the cold. I looked at him, aghast. What had we done? Exhausted, I found my seat, put my head on the table and remained in that position until we reached London, apart from once, when I looked out of the window to see a young woman with light brown hair and a dress the colour of rain standing at the side of the track. I blinked: she was gone.

My new, post-Cardiff life: a basement flat in Brixton; a postgraduate course and, soon, a different set of friends. How clever of me to engineer a new start, one that was almost immediately horribly lonely. I'd only been there a few days when, up the road in Clapham, Angela Carter, whose illuminating, outrageous words steered me through my teenage years and beyond, died of lung cancer aged fifty-one. It seemed symbolic.

Rosa appeared regularly: on escalators, in crowds, just ahead, sideways on. At the Ritzy cinema in Brixton I watched Krzysztof Kieślowski's newly released *The Double Life of Véronique*. Two identical young women, one Polish, one French: one dies, one lives. The whole metaphysical nature of the film, with its unearthly, soaring music, ecstatic emotions and intrinsic sense of aloneness, would have a lasting effect on me. In an extraordinary, unnerving shot, the dead Weronika, struck down mid-song during a concert, looks up through the window of her coffin and the depths of her grave at the faces of the mourners and the azure sky above; her last sight of the world obliterated by the clods of earth which soon obscure the glass.

That summer, Nick graduated along with several of our – or my – former friends. He and I had reconciled by Easter: being apart at that time in our lives was still more unendurable than being together. He came to live with me in London. Instead of accompanying him to attend his graduation ceremony in Cardiff, I stayed behind, as I had a job interview. In a way it was a relief.

I would visit Cardiff only twice more. In early 1994 an old friend from my seminar group invited me to stay. She was studying for a master's in journalism and despite my misgivings I agreed. The weekend was a blur of wrongness. Together with confident, opinionated and mostly male student journalists – not a Welsh accent among them – we piled into the Tafarn. The print of a cherubic curly-haired Dylan Thomas, painted by Augustus John, remained in pride of place on the wall, Guns N' Roses 'Sweet Child O' Mine' still played on the jukebox – but nothing else was the same. Searching for the ghosts of the recent past in all the nooks and crannies, I found them to be absent. The next morning, I made my excuses and caught an earlier train back to London.

In early February 2006 – almost fourteen years since the day of my departure in 1992 – I travelled to Cardiff to meet a man I had begun seeing, a journalist, over from Dublin for a press event. February in Cardiff was bracingly cold, lit by very bright sunshine, but without a hint of spring. Liam was not at all interested in my tales of university life, but obligingly allowed me to take him on The Tour. Later that evening, after dinner, he suggested a nightcap – where should we go? We were in a restaurant in St Mary's Street and instinctively I led us to nearby Quay Street and the Model Inn. Named after Cromwell's New Model Army, it had been one of the places where we'd hung out as students. It was also, although I didn't mention this to Liam, the last pub Rosa visited the night she died.

It was a Monday evening – the pub was almost empty. We drank a glass of red wine each, made small talk. The following day, after he had flown back to Ireland and I was boarding the train for London, I deliberately didn't turn and glance back at the city. During the next decade of my relationship with Liam, he would encourage me to live in the present, not the past.

I had seen Meinir once more, in, the summer of 1993, eighteen months after I had left Cardiff. We had kept in touch intermittently; Meinir was always pragmatic. She was in London for a training course. We had some items to exchange, and met on St Martin's Lane for a coffee after I had finished work, at the Aroma café near the Coliseum: I was addicted to its rainbow-coloured cups and petal-shaped saucers, its tiny *pastéis de nata*. Our talk was breezy, desultory, of people and places that now seemed far behind me, like a film I once saw, the sequence of which I couldn't quite remember.

Afterwards, we walked through Trafalgar Square in the direction of Whitehall and my bus stop. We hugged, made promises to write; assurances which neither of us would keep.

Those were not tears misting my eyes as I turned away to catch the bus south. Merely a fine spray of droplets, unfurling from the nearby fountains.

Epilogue

The cars swoop past behind me, down an otherwise deserted Montague Street as I pause at the eastern entrance to the General Cemetery. It is 5 o'clock in the evening, early November. Drizzling. Damp. Not too cold – the seasons aren't as predictable as they were thirty-seven years ago, when I stood here with my classmates. My first visit to Sheffield for a year, the first since my mother died.

The gravestones which lined the path immediately ahead have gone now, flattened into a park where dogs are walked and children play. There is a Trust and a conservation group, which has in recent years rescued and restored the derelict Grade II chapel, designed by Samuel Worth for the cemetery's opening in 1836, when the cemetery was then 'a remote and undisturbed place'. Now the chapel operates as a venue for weddings, concerts, exhibitions, film screenings. George Partington's stone helmet from the Crimean War has been on show here. The grand Egyptian-themed gatehouse will eventually double up as an Airbnb. Through the trees, on the other side of the high walls which run alongside Frog Walk, I can see a new housing development.

A sour tang, unmistakable, unshakeable since I first chanced upon the cemetery back in 1980, remains in the air. Something sealed up, opened briefly to let in a crack from a second, unearthly world. One that palpates alongside ours.

The nineteenth-century tombs, adorned with melodramatic urns and grieving angels, still stand. The spire of the church – which, unlike the chapel, remains unused and abandoned – rises up like a question mark: a broken, blackened fingernail. Among the prominent steelwork owners and their grand monuments are milliners, anvil-makers, a major Chartist leader, a Black actor from Philadelphia and myriad others. One burial site holds the largest common grave in the country: it contains the remains of ninety-six paupers. The holly trees and oriental planes give them shelter. At the height of summer, red poppies and blue cornflowers undulate amid the grass sighing gently over the paths and catacombs.

Just up the road is my destination, my sister's house, not too far to go. Light, warmth, tea. It has been a long day. But I don't move because I am held back in another time. There was something I conspicuously failed to do here. A task that must be carried out. A dare from long ago. The schoolgirls huddled at the entrance in the fading light, a serial killer on the loose.

Are you frit? I jump; a teasing voice still lingers in the air. Yes, I am frit. I allow a well of self-pity to rise up, then quash it down. *Let it go*, insists the Porter Brook river to my right, flowing in and out of time, as if carrying the emotional detritus of the years to a different, better place.

The past is here, held in this spot reserved for the dead. It is carefully maintained, like the dreams I have of my childhood home – the house empty, the wallpaper curling and rotted, the damp seeping through, condensation streaming down like tears. A black hulk breathes stertorously in the recesses of the cellar, inching its way up the stairs. Someone is trying to enter through the back door to the kitchen and I am unable to lock the door in time, my fingers too stiff, the key not turning. The light switches do not work, I am left in the impossible dark. Waiting.

Here, in the dusk or twilight – I still do not know the difference – the past is present.

'Fancy coming home and being sick!' my father is sitting on the end of my bed. I am unwell, we have just returned from New Zealand. It is the last time I remember him there, in my bedroom. I stood sobbing at the foot of his own bed, in the hospice, two hours after he died. I hadn't seen him for six years. One eye was still partly open, looking at nothing; his face had already developed a waxy sheen. I wanted to kiss him goodbye but was too afraid.

As I look out of the dining-room window, Nina Simone's version of 'Here Comes the Sun' turns on the record player. My mother is lying asleep on the orange sun lounger in the back garden, the Sunday paper fallen to one side. A rare moment of relaxation. Soon she will jump up, bustle about the kitchen, make a batch of scones for tea. The Kenwood mixer will be thrumming. I can smell the scones now, emerging soft and golden from the oven. She is singing.

Over in Chelsea Park, a book of poems lies half open on an abandoned swing, moving slowly, creakingly in the wind whipping up from the elm trees. Rain spatters and stains its pages.

By the cemetery chapel, two Sobranie cigarettes are glowing in the semi-darkness, accompanied by the laughter of a couple of teenage girls, illicitly smoking and drinking on the steps. I can almost taste the sting of their pilfered whisky on my breath.

An unwelcome face looms in front of me, the black hair, the neatly cut beard of photo-fits, newspaper photographs, of lasting nightmares. I dismiss it; other faces are more important than his. The faces of the stalked, the assaulted, the abducted, the murdered.

The cemetery is not safe after dark, was never safe. Thefts are common, muggings, indecent exposures, even a rape has been reported. Flagstones and mementoes have literally been lifted from the grounds and the graves.

Are you frit? That challenge again, echoing through the trees, lobbed at me from the path up ahead. The night coming in fast gleams like pewter. *Mardy bum!* The old Sheffield insult of playgrounds past, present and future.

Dimly I make out a disembodied ponytail, taunting, shining, swinging, pointing the way.

I have experienced everything a person must experience. Christa Wolf, in the guise of Cassandra, in the guise of me.

'*Be strong, dear,*' my mother's voice says, small yet resolute. It was one of the last phrases she spoke.

An invisible hand pushes me firmly forward into the cemetery. I trip and fall heavily on my knees. My tights rip.

There is a roaring in my ears like a banshee.

Is that a kingfisher, blue and green, flashing past?

The halcyon days are coming.

I pick myself up and start to run.

Sources and further reading

Acker, Kathy, *Blood and Guts in High School* (Grove Press, 1984)

Barker, Pat, *Blow Your House Down* (Virago Press, 1984)

Beynon, Huw (editor) *Digging Deeper: Issues in the Miners' Strike* (Verso Books, 1985)

Bowen, Elizabeth, *The Demon Lover and Other Stories* (Jonathan Cape, 1945)

Burn, Gordon, *Somebody's Husband, Somebody's Son: The Story of the Yorkshire Ripper* (Faber & Faber, 1984)

Carter, Angela, *The Magic Toyshop* (Heinemann, 1967)

Dickinson, Peter, *The Changes: A Trilogy* (Gollancz, 1975)

Drabble, Margaret, *The Millstone* (Weidenfeld & Nicolson, 1965)

Gardner, Brian (editor), *Up the Line to Death: War Poets 1914–1918* (Methuen, 1964)

Gee, Maggie, *Grace* (Weidenfeld & Nicolson, 1988)

Godden, Rumer, *The Greengage Summer* (Macmillan & Co., 1958)

Hautzig, Deborah, *Hey, Dollface!* (Greenwillow Books, 1978)

Hines, Barry, *A Kestrel for a Knave* (Michael Joseph, 1968)

Hoy, Linda, *The Damned* (Bodley Head, 1983)

Orwell, George, *Nineteen Eighty-Four* (Secker & Warburg, 1949)

Sheffield City Archives

Smith, Joan, *Misogynies* (Faber & Faber, 1989)

Smith, Patti, *Babel* (G.P. Putnam's Sons, 1978)

Thompson, Dorothy (editor), *Over Our Dead Bodies: Women Against the Bomb* (Virago Press, 1983)

Uttley, Alison, *A Traveller in Time* (Faber & Faber, 1939)

Wolf, Christa, *Cassandra: A Novel and Four Essays*, translated by Jan Van Heurck (Virago Press, 1984)

Woolf, Virginia, *The Voyage Out* (Duckworth, 1915)

226

Acknowledgements

I am very grateful to the Society of Authors for the Authors' Foundation grant which enabled me to finish this book.

My editor Lettice Franklin and all at W&N, Orion, and Hachette UK; my agent Eleanor Birne and all at PEW Literary.

Karolina Sutton and Rebecca Carter for invaluable advice at an early stage.

In January 2021 *Granta* published a version of the chapter that appears in the book as 'Winter Kills'. Thank you to Luke Neima and the online team.

My beloved family and in particular my sister and two brothers. Aspects of our shared past are painful: I appreciate you understanding why I felt compelled to write about them.

Sheffield co-conspirators, some of whom appear in the pages of this book:

Sonia Misak, Alex Henderson, Fiona Simic, and Kieron Rackley.

Celia and Frederick Burgan, in loving memory.

My late stepfather, Ned Irish.

Andrew Goodwin, 1956–2013.

Dr Nigel Bax and all the NHS workers who have, over many years, tried to improve my chronic health issues.

Cathy Marriott, Emma Booker, Caroline Cooper, Parvesh Chhibber, Peter Witchell, Sarah Castleton: dear friends.

With special thanks and love to Cathy and to Judith Rassmann for the quiet space I needed to work on the book's final stages.

Gwendoline Riley, Sunjeev Sahota, Richard Beard, and Will Eaves for all the writerly encouragement.

Michael Caines, Daniela Petracco, Marta Alonso, Robert Fiszer (and Carmen and Eliot) for being there.

My amazing mother, Pearl, died in 2016. I remember her every day with gratitude and love.

Catherine Taylor, January 2023